A Note from the Publisher

I am deeply indebted to my friend Pratap Nambiar without whose perseverance and guidance this work would not have been completed. It was his firm conviction that his grand uncle's writing on GANESHA needed a much wider audience that has resulted in this – our first publishing venture. We hope you enjoy it.

CREDITS

Picture Credits:
Jewelkraft, Bombay
R.K. Studios, Chembur, Bombay
Karan Kapoor, Bombay
M/s. Mitter Bedi, Bombay
Shree Sai Graphics

Acknowledgement:
Mr. Rayasam H. Sharma

Graphic Designing: Jaiprakash Tiwari

Printed at: Rashmi Printers, Bombay-12.

Ashtavinayaka Illustrations: Manoj Pal

Back Cover: Ganesha in Cloth

First Published in 1992
Second Impression 1992
Third Impression 1995
Fourth Impression 2000

Published by:
Book
Quest *publishers*
21, Rajgir Chambers, 12/14,
Shahid Bhagat Singh Road,
Opp. Old Customs House,
Bombay - 400 023, INDIA.
Email: bookquestpub@yahoo.com
        bookchannel@vsnl.com

ISBN 81-86025-00-6

PREFACE

*T*his book is presented to the readers with a foreword by His Holiness Dr. E. Nandiswara Nayake Thero. The author made it clear that His Holiness' wisdom shall prevail over that of the author in the assessment of the typescript.

Mahatma Gandhi said, "God is not a person but an immutable law and in this the law and the maker are one".

Buddha called this immutable law as Dharma. Christ called it as Eloi the Will of his Father in heaven. Mohammed called it as Allah a word related to El and Eloi. Einstein called it as the cosmic law, Douglas Fawcet referred to it as cosmic Intelligence, Spinoza illustrated the law by saying "two apples added to two apples make four". Any amount of prayer or pious wish will not make it five. Even God will not countenance such a move.

Ganesha obviously is a design likewise meant to convey a profound meaning. But owing to the play of ignorance a good deal of ritualism has sprung up around him clouding the meaning of his design and form. This is unfair and it behoves one and all who is in search of knowledge to probe into the deeper meaning behind Ganesha's funny form.

The author offers his sincere thanks to Mr. Howard Murphet the learned author of 'Sai Baba — Man of Miracles' for suggesting the title for this book.

This book is placed in the hands of the readers by the author in all humility as a humble tribute to Ganesha.

Rankorath Karunakaran
Author

"SAI NIVAS"
24, Five Furlongs Road,
Guindy, Chennai 600 032.

FOREWARD

By H.H. Dr. E. Nandiswara Nayake Thero
Director
MAHA BODHI SOCIETY, CHENNAI.

I have been aware of the activities of the Author Sri R. Karunakaran, B.A., B.L., as a Member of the Bar, a Member of the Theosophical Society, for the past several years and a researcher in the schools of Indian Philosophy. His present task in this light work has been to give a perspective of ancient cult, the Ganesha cult, prevalent from the earliest times in the sub-continent and the Indians have carried it to farther shores of Asia and even South America. The elephant was a symbol of majesty and strength and determination in early iconography. In the animal kingdom it was symbolical of rank, sagacity and profound intelligence. It was also remarkable for its purity of habits. Its food too is pure vegetarian. Though gregarious in habit, it nevertheless commanded monarchical ascendancy over all animals.

The elephant's precedence of astute intelligence was accepted by early man. It was in recognition of this remarkable calibre and sense of propriety that the royal elephant was entrusted with the task of selecting a successor to the throne, in the event of a demise of a monarch without a real heir. In ancient India, the numerical superiority of the army was in accordance with the strength of the elephant force. King Bimbisara of Maghadha had an army of 5,000 elephants and King Pasandi of Khosala had an equally strong army of elephants. The superiority of the clansmen was reckoned on the number of elephants that clansmen held. The second and third degree of prestige in clansmen were the numerical superiority of the equestrian and cattle holdings. Thus in early society the pride of worldly possession was given to the elephant. The master of the largest kraal of elephants commanded the highest respect in primeval society. The possession of a white tusker by any monarch was a symbol of ethereal favour, and wordly prosperity in the kingdom. This was a feature in India, Burma, Thailand, Cambodia and Sri Lanka. The elephant was deemed as a Rathna (jewel) and was adored as one of the seven jewels of monarchical luck.

The birth of a white elephant in a kingdom was a rarity and such a birth ushered in an era of prosperity and plentitude in the land. The birth of Prince Sidhartha in the human world severing his connection with the Tusita heaven, was after the assumption of the shape of a white baby elephant. Tradition states that Maha Mayadevi dreamt that a lustrous silver elephant magnificent in its grace descended from the clouds upon a silver peak and approached the Queen and she felt that, piercing her right side with its shining tusks and that the elephant entered her womb. The white elephant was a symbol of purity and perfection.

The elephant in accordance with folk lore are of several noble families. The Culla

Hathi, Padopama and the Maha Hathi Padopama Suttas identify seven families of elephant. The 'Kanoon', 'Naga' and 'Halthi' are common terms used in Pali language to identify an elephant. Dandhi-Tusker has been used in terms of an elephant with tusks only. Nontuskers were not engaged in warfare nor on ceremonial occasions. They were relegated for labour and were not considered as noble. The elephant was valued according to its majesty, of its height and the length and grace of its tusks. If the tusks were milky white and parallel and have equal length gracefully protruding, reaching a length of seven to twelve feet, such a royal animal was greatly valued. Very often the colour of its skin too mattered. The whiter the skin, the greater the appreciation. The jathaka tales specify that 'Chata danta kala' is the noblest in the family of elephants. These magnificent animals are supposed to have reached forty feet height in ancient India and bragged of a pair of tusks exceeding 18 feet in length. Probably, these must have been the last family of the prehistoric mammoths. The elephant was a symbol embodying many qualities — royalty, benignity, prudence and compassion. The worshipper of Ganesha adores not the figure but the qualities symbolised by the elephant's head.

The serpent girdle of Ganesha worn around the loins or in certain figures as an additional embellishment of a sacred thread suspended from the left shoulder is again a significant deviation. The Naga, the hooded cobra was an emblem of totemistic worship among the earliest jungle dwellers; though its venom was deadly, yet the reptile was sacred, as primitive man visualised a divine agency in the appearance of cobra. Superstitious rituals were performed to propitiate the provocation of the Naga. In early Buddhist texts reference is made to the Naga and its various communities. In the 'Kandha Paditha' mention is made of as many as twelve families of Nagas. These cobras are supposed to have bred in communities. The earliest forest dwellers of the Indian Community that migrated to the Indo-Gangetic and Indo-Brahmaputra valleys worshipped the Naga and they were also identified as Nagas. The Buddha encountered this community of Nagas in the valley of the Narmada. They were at that time adorers of the serpents and the seven hooded Naga and the amorous clasp of the male and female cobra were forms of totems they worshipped. When the Buddha converted them to the fold of Buddhists, they abandoned their animistic worship and requested the Buddha for a form of enlightened worship. Then the Buddha imprinted his left foot on the banks of Narmada and asked them to grace the foot of the Buddha.

The earliest Aryans in the Euphrates, Tigris and Nile Valleys resorted to Naga worship and the same Aryans that settled in the river valleys of Bharat associated the visit of the Naga with the reflections of dead ancestors. Frequency of such visits compelled them to conduct pooja to propitiate the dead who now had visited them in the form of cobras. These ancient ancestors that now visited were welcome guests and afforded food in forms of milk, rice and eggs and implored to leave them after blessing them. The ancients were particular to avoid curse of the serpents. These were never killed but courteously coaxed to leave; if ever one

In Bronze (Three metal B, C, Z) crawling Ganesha, from Kumbakonam, Tamilnadu.

Playful Ganesha

callously destroyed a cobra, the ignorant villagers attributed all inclemencies of weather and failure of crops to such a wanton act of the community, as the weather Gods had rebelled against them due to the wrath of the ancestors.

The same serpent that some times was reckoned as a harbinger of goodwill was reckoned as an evil omen that brought them curse of Gods on certain occasions. All semitic civilisations have associated the visit of the viper with curses of God. It is perhaps this fear of the serpent power that incited them to adopt some form of the reptile in the sphere of wordly power symbolically. The Indian pantheon of ideological Deities have all embraced the hooded cobra. Cobra reliefs are prominently portrayed in all columns of Hindu Temples.

The Buddhists and Jains too have associated the cobra (Naga) with remarkable powers of discretion. Saints are protected by them and the purity of the saint is vouchsafed by them. Hence the wisdom of the Naga supercedes man's. The Naga is a Symbol of purity in the Pali language. The aspirant for higher ordination brought before the Sangha is named the Naga implying one without faults, absolved purified one, befitting one, etc. The Vammika Sutta mentions the discovery of the Naga at the bottom of the pit in the excavation of the mound "Do not harm the Naga; it is fully absolved, cleaned one; its state is that of perfection." Thus the state of Arhat hood-perfect saint-the jeevan mukta has been associated with State of Naga. In the Uraga Vagga of the Sutta Nipata and the Naga Vagga of Dhammapada, many a description is found based upon the Naga or Serpent. In Sanyutta Nikaya, Mara assumes the form of a deadly cobra puffing flames and smoke.

Thus religious schools both Indian and foreign have associated the Cobra with the purest and the heinous. What one may attribute to be necklace or girdle of serpents in the figure of the elephant trunked Hindu Deity is to be understood in accordance with the motive for which he is worshipped.

Ganesha is supposed to ride upon a mouse. It is strange that Ganesha the Lord of Wisdom has been granted most dissimilar and disproportionate attributes in the world when his brother Kumar has been accorded a noble bird like the peacock as his vehicle. Parvathi's son is granted a humble obsequious mouse quite incapable of lifting the bulging belly and massive head that he possesses. Does it imply that wisdom is an attribute of ugly conglomeration of factors or that the wise do not find anything in the world disproportionate or ugly?

The mouse symbolises hidden life in the atom. The spark of fire that is vibrant in every living phenomena. Agni that assumed the form of a mouse is that atomic energy which is procreation of life. Even as fire is a faithful servant but a bad master, the mouse is both creative and destructive, therefore it is kept under the footstool of the Master. This feature could be attributed to the task of nirmana and pralaya of Shiva, the father of Ganesha. Shiva creates and destroys; but is also capable of maintaining his creation in trim. The obsequious rat, the great elephant, the powerful man and the crawling reptile are cross sections of the Nirmana Sakti of Shiva. These were personified in Ganesha, the son of Parvathi, even in the absence of Iswara, the Creator. Here again, the potential evidence of the Sakti is revealed in magnificence.

Shiva in the form of linga or Shakti in the form of Ambal the Universal Mother, is a primitive cult that goes back to the earliest Dravidians of Mohanjodaro and Harappa cultures. His place was Supreme in South India and he was patronised by the ruling class. The plebians of the south adopted the crude composition of Ganesha as more proximate to an agrarian populace. His wisdom, his compassion, his steadfast non-frivolous nature and his pot belly significant of the bounty of nature all appealed to their crude mind.

Vinayaka is a name given to Ganesha. The Lord Buddha is called Vinayaka as he had the singular power to bring under control those that are uncontrollable; the tractor of untractable. Whether Ganesha was endowed with such powers of curbing the indocile is not clear in the history of his cult; but Vinayaka in Hindu Pantheon signifies the chitta visuddhi endowing the knowledge of liberation. This clarity of knowledge is obtainable through yoga alone.

The author has vividly and cogently identified the Pancha Makara Thathwa of the Shakti cult and stripped it of the licentious interpretation given at the hands of fanatics who had no understanding of the inner spiritual methods and engaged to demean lofty thought with obscene wordly renderings.

Lobsang Rampa in his book 'the third eye' refers to the intelligent eye that is opened under the pursuit of higher meditation. Tibetan mystics paid the highest respect to the enlightenment through the mystic third eye. The two natural eyes exposed worldly consciousness; the super normal eye opened vistas of realms beyond the reach of the average man. Ganesha's third eye is the symbol of this supramundane knowledge he is said to be endowed with.

The term 'OM', has been used in all Hindu literature Sanskrit and Dravidian. All schools of Hinduism accept 'OM', as indicative of purity and divinity. The main fact remains that all meditation in Hinduistic schools resort to 'OM', as a primary source of intelligence leading to Brahma Vidya. The four states Turya, Sushupta, Swapna and Jagratha are conditions existing upon the stream of consciousness. Consciousness is alert from birth till death. There is consciousness vigilant even in deep sleep. Man may slumber in deep forgetfulness but consciousness never sleeps.

Shiva's role as the patron of yogis is a duty assigned to him long before he became Kapala Iswara or Nata Raja. These qualities of Shiva are attributes assigned to him by Dravidians. The earlier Aryan Brahmins disrespected him sheerly because the Dravidian plebians worshipped him. Even after Shiva gained a permanent place in the Pantheon, Ganesha was laughed at by Aryan Brahmins. It was just fifteen centuries ago that Ganesha was able to make his impact felt in the North.

Ganesha was created out of the body Chandana Scrubbings of his mother and Shiva that severed his young head implanted the elephant head with the proboscis trunk and tusks. Yet he is imperishable, stainless, unconditioned, of transcending omkar and of supreme bliss. These are qualities that arise from deep meditation equating to the state of jivan muktas. Therefore, Ganesha is symbolical of the finite perfection of man in his supreme ascendance to liberation from birth. Therefore, one that worships Ganesha should aspire for this perfection in him.

The writer in his chapter on psychic centres refers to Muladharam the base of mental action. The psychic cynosure is neither the base of the spine nor the heart. It is the brain, the base of the cognition series. Ganesha in the early days was the patron of music and fine art. Prior to the era that Shiva assumed the role as patron of music and dance, in his pose of Nataraja, Ganesha was invoked as the presiding Deity of knowledge culture and fine art. Just as Ganesha was the brain child of the artist, he presided over the brain of the art student. Yoga was the highest art of frail humanity in the quest of perfection; therefore Ganesha's invocation at the beginning of yogic adventure requesting him to guide the student was an accepted norm.

Ganesha cult was a primitive cult among the Dravidians of the prehistoric era. The early Aryan invaders did not accept the Dravidian Gods, but degraded them. At a later stage the renegaded Deities were uplifted to the united Hindu Pantheon. The Indian whether Aryan or Dravidian was an idol worshipper. Ganesha symbolised unity of the primaeval forest denizen with man, the majesty of the elephant combining the physical energy of the homosapiens. The Dravidian Saiva cult was much older than the evolution of Ganesha. Therefore, the Dravidian made Ganesha, the son of Shiva but subsequent bhaktas have made an effort to make Shiva, a creation of Ganesha, with the avowed purpose of reviving the universal mother who was a more magnificent personality in Dravidian culture. The Amman worship prevails to this day, pursued mainly by the labour and working communities.

Hindu mythology has undergone varying vicissitudes in the centuries. Once Ganesha was a popular Deity. Subsequently, he is stripped of his powers and relegated to secondary importance as son of Shiva created by Parvathi. He became a plebian Deity and subsequently is exalted into the Pantheon enjoying equal status with Shiva and Parvathi and takes precedence over his playful younger brother, Kumar. He guides Kumar through his higher intellectual powers and some times outwits him.

However time has preserved him and custom has not slowed his worship. This cult of worship has spread to foreign climes and he is endorsed as the patron of learning in all Eastern countries however grotesque his figure may be. It has been a custom in many an Eastern land to offer rituals to Ganesha before a child reads his first letters.

Ganesha is primarily a sober non-sexprovoked Deity and therefore it is sheer corruption to associate him with the physical Goddesses, Siddhi, Buddhi and Vallabha. Siddhi and Buddhi are qualities of Ganesha personified as Goddesses. They are not his wives but his votaries. Vallabha may have the consolation of a consort; but this is a vulgar depiction at a later corrupted stage of the cult of Ganesha worship and the obscenity bereft Ganesha of his virtues and the cult itself declined.

In Buddha's images in Nepal and Tibet, two Goddesses Karuna and Maitri are placed by the side of the main image. The Buddha is a parama vairagy and it is sheer absurdity to place Goddesses besides his figure. However, the artist had no power to express the exuberance of love and kindness in the Buddha. Therefore, they brought in the figure of two Goddesses, Karuna and Maitri, symbolically. They stand forever symbolical characteristics of the Buddha, in the same manner, Siddhi and Buddhi are symbolical virtues of Ganesha worshipped by the devotee. Siddhi is symbolical of the mystic powers and Buddhi, the wisdom.

Though the Ganesha cult spread to South East Asiatic countries, it did not survive long there and it is quite possible that the early Indian traders took Vinayaka with them to Mexico. There is evidence of early Indian impact upon Mexico though it is not historic.

Like all other vigrahas, the idol of Ganesha has undergone divergent vicissitude but it has survived to an enlightened age of science. Tradition dies hard in Hinduism. Therefore the worship of Ganesha shall pervade into the next millenniums emanating in his crude lustre symbolising the echo of the final animal in grotesque man. The major fact remains, though millenniums rolled by, man yet remains closer to animal today than he was ever before.

Ganesha had his appeal to primitive man who failed to apprehend the ulterior motivation of symbols. Crude symbols were attributed with nobler significance by understanding man. Here, the worship became meaningful but fear of the grotesque appearance faded away into amorous adoration. Adoration paved the way for esoteric sublimation. Ganesha even today is worshipped by all three types of devotees.. The multi facets of his physiognomy and the exuberance of his physique are meaningful and thought provoking.

Mind is the precursor of matter. Mind predominates over all correlative matter. The mind is indivisible even so is matter its correlative. The fundamental arising in the world is absolutely prompted by the mind alone. Mind creates, procreates, equalises, distributes, attributes, co-responds and finally destroys matter. Though mind is capable of creating, evoking and dissolving matter, matter never has the capacity of producing a mind. Thus, mind takes precedence over the strata of matter. In the Dhammapada, we read, all elements arise out of the mind, they have the mind as their cynosure and spontaneously goaded by the mind alone they are shaped. Mind is a product of time, experience and consciousness. One may argue that mind is a part of the universal consciousness; therefore it is eternal. All matter undergoes innovation as universal flux is the dire nature of matter. Mind that creates matter itself is constantly changing. Therefore, neither matter nor the mind its creator is constant. All matter conditioned by the mind is subjected to the flux of change. Therefore both mind and matter are non-eternal.

The writer's approach is analytical and argumentative. I hope his readers would appreciate his efforts made in tracing the history of Ganesha cult and Worship.

Dr. E. Nandiswara Nayake Thero
Director

MAHA BODHI SOCIETY,
17, Kenneth Lane,
Chennai - 600 008.

About the Author

*T*he author Rankorath Karunakaran hails from Elapulli, a village of Palghat District in Kerala. He was born on 30th January 1904 in a Nair family.

After graduating from Madras Law College he started practising in Madras itself. During World War II, he served as a Volunteer Home Guard Officer. It was during this time that he came in contact with Mr. L.G. Banks, an Englishman who invited him to work as a Legal Officer in his firm, a post which he continued till his retirement.

After his retirement he became a member of Theosophical Society. He developed an interest in Philosophy and became a member of the Madras University Library where he spent most of his time. This place was his inspiration for writing this book. The author is at present working on another book, 'Chips and Charcoal from Bharath' which is pending release.

His family consists of his wife, seven children and a younger sister.

CONTENTS

॰॥ विघ्नेश्वराय गणनाथ नमो नमस्ते ॥॰

GANESHA THE SUMUKHA

*T*he elephant-faced-Deity of the Hindus known popularly as Ganesha has intrigued all thinking men all over the world, all through the ages even unto the present day. They are puzzled as to how a cultured class of people going by the name of Hindus could have denigrated themselves by worshipping this funny looking elephant-faced-Deity giving him an eminent status in their pantheon.

You go anywhere in India you will find him in the Hindu temples, thoroughfares, public parks, pavements, bathing ghats and even on hill tops and wherever the Hindus went they took with them this Deity and secured for him a status not less than what he held in the country of his origin.

Besides India, Tibet and Nepal, he is also found in almost all countries in South East Asia and even in China and Japan. It is surprising to note that in the distant Mexico the cult of Ganesha was prevalent as is revealed by his figures discovered in the archaeological excavations in that country. Recently, in U.S.A. also a Ganesha temple was consecrated at Flushing, a suburb of New York.

The reverence and devotion for him in India and also elsewhere have not abated even in these days of free thinking and rationalism. He is invoked by all classes of orthodox Hindus in all walks of life for success in their endeavours and thanked profusely after success.

In an elated state of mind a high ranking Hindu Naval Officer is reported to have broken 108 coconuts before the image of this Deity in an unofficial thanksgiving ceremony for his victory in a naval engagement over the Pakistan Navy in the 1971 war.

The action of this Officer may look silly and superstitious, but one cannot condemn it like that. The Officer hails from a cultured community and he, emulating his ancestors, would not have done this if he or his ancestors had not discovered something sublime in this grotesque figure.

In an article published in Femina - March 25 - April 7, 1977 Kamini Kaushal makes a reference to her conversation with Pertrushka, a Russian girl in Moscow, who reveals that her husband Ivan, a Physics Engineer is a great Yoga fan, practising yoga every morning. She also reveals that Ganesha is his favourite God and that to please her husband she has to give up smoking and drinking. As in the case of the Hindu Naval Officer, the young Moscow Engineer also appears to have discovered the sublime in the image of Ganesha.

Ganesha is usually depicted either as a pictograph or as an idol with the body of a man deformed by a big belly and disproportionate limbs with the head of an elephant, having only one tusk, the other tusk appearing broken. He wears a serpent girdle either across his shoulder or around his belly. In some images he is seen with two heads. There are also three headed Ganeshas, four headed Ganeshas and five headed Ganeshas. In certain images he is seen with a third eye in his forehead.

Although he is reputed to be a celibate he is seen in certain depictions with his two platonic consorts Buddhi (Wisdom) and Siddhi (the mystic power) and amazingly the entire weight of this bizarre figure with the two consorts is mounted on a tiny mouse.

In the mythologies of other countries we have similar figures with human bodies and animal heads. Asshur, the chief Assyrian God, had a bird's head. Horus, the Chief Egyptian God, had a falcon's head. Another Egyptian God, Anubis, had a jackal's head. The Egyptian Goddess Sekhmet had a lion's head. Minos, the Greek God had a bull's head and Hera the Greek Goddess had a cow's head.

In Indian mythology, besides Ganesha, we have Deities like Varahamurthy with the head of a boar, Narasimhamurthy with the head of a lion and Hayagrivamurthy with the head of a horse. But in no mythology could anyone find a Deity like Ganesha as an object of daily worship as by the orthodox Hindus.

 There are about ninety one different figures of Ganesha according to the estimate of research scholars. The details of their make up vary from figure to figure with no change in the main set up. It is in the enigma of certain striking variations in detail that the sublime in the figures of Ganesha has to be sought for.

Some figures are seen standing; some are seen in a dancing pose; some are seen sitting with trunks turning towards the left side invariably reaching a bowl of modaka (a sweet edible preparation). In some figures the trunks are seen turning towards right and in some straight hanging down with or without a pot of nectar in the curve of their trunks.

In some images he is seen standing, resting his right foot on a lion and his left foot on a mouse. In some other images his left foot is found resting on a mouse and his right foot lifted in an effort to touch the serpent girdle, his mount carrying a jewel in its mouth.

According to the strict rules of Hindus iconography, Ganesha figures with only two hands are taboo. This rule is however waived by Vigneshwara Prathistha Vidhi (rules for installing Vigneshwara idols). Vigneshwara is another name for Ganesha. Ganesha figures are generally seen with four hands which signify their divinity. Some figures are seen with six, some with eight, some with ten, some with twelve, some with fourteen hands, each hand carrying a symbol which

differs from the symbols in other hands, there being about fiftyseven symbols in all, according to the findings of research scholars.

Three animals viz, the elephant, the serpent and the mouse have contributed for the make up of the figures of Ganesha. The elephant has contributed for his head, the serpent for his girdle and the mouse for his mount.

When you look at this funny figure, it looks as though the fragile mouse is made to carry the heavy head and bloated belly of the Deity with the serpent girdle, in perpetual fear of the serpent, aggressively poised within striking distance, which may appear to be nothing short of a piece of iconographic vagary. In spite of this vagary Ganesha is addressed reverentially as Sumukha meaning 'He of good face.'

Ganesha being a composite image we have to study the parts involved in his make up to understand the concept behind his image, how it was evolved and what it stands for.

Shri Ballaleshwar – Pali

GANESHA AND THE ELEPHANT

Ganesha is not a Deity of the vedic pantheon. In one of the seals discovered in archaeological excavations at Mohanjodaro and Harappa of the Indus Valley, there is the find of a figure of a ram with a human face and trunk and tusks of an elephant.

Thattiriya Aranyaka refers to a Deity called Dentin (one with tusk) who is said to possess a twisted trunk (Vakrathunda). It is not clear whether this Deity had the full form of the elephant or not. Probably this figure was a mixed figure in the pattern of the earlier figure found in the Indus Valley excavations, viz., the ram with the human face and with the trunk and tusks of the elephant. These figures may be the present day Ganesha figures in their embryonic stage. Significantly enough, only the trunk and tusks of the elephant appear to have been taken out for depiction, perhaps for the reason, that even in that distant past they had a special significance as at the present day. To comprehend the full significance of these trunk and tusks we have to study the significance of the elephant, an animal existing side by side with human beings from the very prehistoric day.

The elephant may have been a totem animal during the prehistoric period. Potemism is supposed to be the earliest appearance of organised religion when the totem animals were worshipped. Some times totem animals were humanised and given great importance. There is a picture in extent, of a piece of sculpture preserved in Paris museum which was excavated from Western Persia. This sculpture is said to be belonging to a period between 1200 B.C. and 1000 B.C. according to L. Vanden Berghe quoted by Fr. H. Heras.

This sculpture contains the figure of a man dressed in old Persian attire with the head of an elephant with its trunk turned inward towards its mouth brandishing a sword in one hand while the other hand holds the tail of a serpent crawling towards his feet. If the date ascribed to this find is correct it affords proof that this totem figure was humanised during the period immediately following the Vedic era when Vedas were still being transmitted by word of mouth. Humanising the totem is a step forward in metaphysics and philosophy also for it is starting point of man creating God heads after his own image or according to his own mental ability and fancies.

Elephants and bulls are the prominent animals seen in the Indus Valley seals. Shiva Lingams are also seen. In one of the seals there is the figure of a naked yogi sitting in Padmasana (Lotus posture) with bracelets on his arms in yogic contemplation. He is surrounded by two antelopes, an elephant, a tiger, a rhinoceros and a buffalo. Shiva is personified as a great yogi. He is also called

Pasupathi which may mean lord of souls and/or lord of beasts and therefore the figure of the yogi in this seal may be surmised as the figure of Shiva. From the several objects found in the excavation of Mohanjodaro and Harappa it is surmised that Shiva was worshipped both in the anthropomorphic and the linga forms. Father Heras has demonstrated that the culture of the ancient Indus Valley was proto Dravidian. We do not know by what name Shiva was called by the people of the ancient Indus Valley and what was the status enjoyed by the elephant. The language spoken by the ancient Indus Valley people was something like Tamil can be proved by Brauhi spoken by the people of Kelat in Baluchistan. Brauhi tongue has its root in Tamil. Father Heras also said that the ancient Dravidians worshipped a God called AN and this god came to be called Shiva or SIVAN in later times. In the Dravidian language the elephant is called ANA and in the light of the studies of Father Heras we can hazard a guess and say that this pachyderm was sacred to AN or at any rate a sacred animal.

The elephants seen in the several seals appear calm and docile in spite of their imposing appearance. They look just like the elephants kept in the Hindu temples for ceremonial purposes at the present time and it looks probable that keeping of elephants in places of worship for ceremonial purpose is a tradition that is being followed from the days of the prehistoric Indus Valley civilization. There may not be anything absurd if we say on ontological consideration that the genesis of Ganesha with his elephantine head can be traced to the entity represented as a yogi and the elephant seen by his side along with other animals in the above referred seal of the Indus Valley.

Ephom is another Indian name of elephant. Elephant is an English Word derived through Greek by adding the prefix 'EL' and the suffix 'Ant' to the 'ephom'. 'EL' is a primitive generic word for God in the semitic language. Even in the Dravidian language 'EL' or 'ELI' indicates God. Ellappan and Ellamman are the names of two Deities and still worshipped in South India, Ellappan being the Father Deity and Ellamman being the Mother Deity.

In the word elephant, the suffix 'Ant' indicates a thing or agency and therefore the word elephant like the Dravidian word 'AN' and its variations like Anai, Ana and Enugu may mean an animal that is god or at least an animal worshipped as a totem or dedicated to 'An' a Dravidian deity later on identified as Shiva.

In the early days of conquest of the Indus Valley, the invading Aryans flushed with pride were bent upon belittling the Deities and sacred animals of the people of the Indus Valley. They ridiculed Shivalingam the pillar emblem of God common among the semitic and Dravidian races as Sisna Deva (Phallus God) and made the holy elephant as the mount for their chief of Gods Indra. To add insult to injury, this elephant mount of Indra was named by the invaders as Iravathan meaning face of God (Ira meaning god and vathan meaning face). Motives of the origin apart, the coining of the word Iravatham is analogous in process and content to the coining of the word 'Pe-ni-el' (face of God) by Jacob to name the place where at he had a night long wrestle with an angel and where at he erected a pillar to commemorate the fight.

The domination and arrogance of the Aryan God did not last long. The elephants regained their lost importance and began to play prominent roles in all affairs where men and God are involved Buddhists also hold these animals sacred, as Lords. Buddha is said to have descended from heaven in the form of a white elephant into his mother's womb in answer to her prayer to Ganesha for a child. When Buddha was recognised as an avathar (incarnation) of Maha Vishnu by the Hindus the status of the elephant also went a step high.

After the Aryan invasion of the Indus Valley many of the original inhabitants migrated to the south carrying their cultural and religious traditions with them. The elephant continued to be their sacred animal, in the South also which is proved by the ancient custom of the Pattathu Anai (State Elephant) selecting a ruler by placing a garland of flowers round his neck. The state elephant was considered as a Divine medium and the people respected its verdict without demur.

The elephant was also considered as a royal symbol besides being considered as a religious symbol both in Hindu and Buddhist countries and was trained for the purpose of war. With the disappearance of princely order and the mechanisation of the army, its importance as a royal symbol and war material suffered a setback. But it still retains its importance as a religious paraphernalia. Apart from its esoteric role in the Hindu metaphysics which is dealt with in the chapters following, it is considered an auspicious animal representing the Phenomenal world. Lakshmi, the Hindu Goddess of prosperity is reverentially addressed as Gajalakshmi. This idea is symbolised in pictures and other works of art with this Goddess flanked on either side by two elephants facing each other with trunks lifted in holy tribute to her.

The symbolic and mystic role of the elephant in human affairs which has been coming down from immemorial past appears to have influenced the gradual evolution of the concept of Ganesha and his idol in the present forms.

The esoteric significance of the word Gajam meaning elephant is explained in Chapter Eleven.

Shri Mahaganpati – Ranjangaon

Ganesha immersion, Chowpatty – Bombay

Bronze Image in Kumbakonam (Tamilnadu)

Yatra Ganesha with umbrella from Tamilnadu

Rosewood and Plastic Inlaid with Base from Mysore

Brass Ganesha from Delhi

GANESHA AND THE SERPENT

*I*n the images and pictorial representations Ganesha is seen wearing a serpent girdle around his waist. In some figures, the serpent is seen sporting across his left shoulder like a sacred thread. This cold blooded reptile gives Ganesha a look of aversion. But this is a meaningful detail which cannot be avoided in his make up. In the set up of one of the seals of the Indus Valley, there is the figure of a yogi flanked on either side by two suppliants with the figure of a serpent standing erect on its tail. The date of this seal may be between 4000 B.C. and 3000 B.C. Similarly in one of the relics of the ancient Mesopotamian civilization there is the find of a goblet used by king Gudea of Lagash in connection with some fertility rite. On this goblet among other figures is seen a figure of two serpents entwined in an amorous embrace. This goblet is said to belong to a period round about 2500 BC.

The serpent standing erect on its tail in the seal of the Indus Valley is probably indicative of the awakening of Kundalini Sakthi (serpent energy) in the yogi as a result of his asceticism. Kundalini Sakthi is the coiled energy lying dormant in all beings which is symbolised as a serpent lying in coils. The entwined serpents seen in the Mesopotamian goblet are probably indicative of the positive and negative or the male and the female principles involved in this energy which is responsible for the appearance of the entire universe. In ancient Mesopotamia the symbol of entwined serpent was also used as the symbol of the God of healing, Ningishizda. This symbol was later on adopted by the Greeks. The Greek God of healing was called Askilapios who was worshipped at two great centres, viz., Rome and Epidaurus. Epidaurus has been called the Lourdes of the ancient world. Sufferers came to this Temple and spent the night there in the darkness. The emblem of Askilapios was a snake.

Accordingly, tame and harmless snakes were let loose in the dormitories. When they wandered and touched the sick people lying there, they thought it was the touch of God and they were healed. The Romans honoured this emblem by the design of caduceus, the staff carried by Mercury the messenger of their Gods. A representation of this staff is used as an emblem by the medical profession all over the world and as the insignia of the U.S. Army Medical Corps. The emblem of entwined serpents is also seen guarding the Holy Cross mounted on the official staff of certain christian church dignitaries consecrated by His Holiness the Patriarch of Antioch. Athena Palias, the Patron Goddess of the City of Athens is depicted in the coins belonging to the First Century B.C. holding a serpent entwined Spear.

The entwined serpent stones are quite common in India even at the present time. Young women are seen going round these stones in silent prayer in the hope of getting married or begetting children. This is in keeping with the spirit of ancient fertility rites wherein the entwined serpent figures were worshipped. The festival of Diasia in honour of God Zeus in ancient Greece was dominated by a Sacred Snake considered as a symbol of underworld powers.

Many look askance at these serpent emblems. But there are enough people who see great esoteric significance in them. The emblem of Manchester University depicts a looped serpent with the rising sun in the background. Certainly the serpent here is not meant to be the evil genius of the University. The Theosophical Society and the Ramakrishna Mission, two cultural and religious organisations have adopted symbols of serpents with heads meeting the tails. The ancient Celts also appear to have used serpent symbols. The Celtic Deity the horned kerunnes is pictured as sitting in a yoga posture holding in his right hand a serpent swallowing its own tail and in his left hand a serpent held by the neck. Just like the horned yogi of the Indus Valley before him, this Deity is also surrounded by animals such as a goat, a stag, a boar and a lion.

The serpent swallowing its own tail, or with head touching its own tail is said to be a symbol of eternity where there is neither beginning not end. The Mithraic cult of ancient Persia had a symbol of seven maidens with serpent heads in white garment. Mithra was Persian God identified with sun and these serpent maidens may be representing the seven rays of the sun, divinised as seven mothers in Hindu mythology. Ancient Cretans also worshipped a Goddess holding a snake in each of her hands. In Hindu Mythology the serpent 'Adisesha', on whose coils God Maha Vishnu rests is an allegorical representation of the Divine aspect of the mind, the lower aspect of which being represented by the Venom spitting Kaliya who was tamed by the grace of Lord Krishna. It may be noted that the concept of Adisesha (beginning and end) which signifies eternity is analogous to the concept of Alpha and Omega propounded by St. John the Divine.

Shiva another God of the Hindu Trinity who is symbolised as the God of Salvation and as a great yogi and who is spoken of as the father of Ganesha is adorned with serpents all over his body as a token of victory by the yogi over the base qualities of his mind. Buddha was said to have been sheltered under the hood of a serpent for seven days during the period of his trance before he attained his Buddhahood. Similarly it is said that Guru Nanak was also sheltered by a serpent with hood spread when he was lying in a trance in an open field. It is said that soon after the birth of Bhagavan Satya Sai Baba a cobra was seen under his bed cloth. The cobra did not do any harm to the child. It is also said that the Sai Baba of Shirdi materialises himself as a serpent before his devotees. The ancient Druids who were the high priests of the Celts are said to be Dravidian yogis. They are referred to as the wise men of the East. They called themselves as serpents or Nagas. Buddha is said to have had contacts with them. Jesus Christ was obviously referring to these wisemen when he told the twelve apostles that they should be wise as serpents and harmless as doves before he sent them out to preach about the kingdom of God.

In ancient Egypt serpent worship was common. It seems to have been based on the idea of the serpent as the good genius of the house and of the temple. In India also this notion was prevalent and it is still lingering among certain orthodox communities who are averse to the killing of cobras. If however a cobra is killed, care is taken to give it a decent cremation. In Egypt, serpent was also regarded as a royal emblem. It was ancient belief that God visited his devotees in the form of serpents. It is said that Alexander, Julius Caesar and other great heroes of olden days had their mothers visited by a serpent before they were conceived.

In the Old Testament of the Bible we have references of Moses throwing down his rod at the behest of God and the rod becoming a serpent and in another context the rod of Aron becoming a serpent and devouring the magician's serpent in a bid for spiritual eminence before the Pharaoh of Egypt. We have also the account of the fiery serpents sent by God to punish the people of Israel when they spoke ill of God and Moses, and the setting up of a Brazen serpent on a pole by Moses at the command of God when he (Moses) interceded on behalf of the repentant people, so that all those who were afflicted by the bite of these fiery serpents may get cured by looking at this Brazen serpent. Esoterically the fiery serpents can be taken as symbols of the lower side of the mind and the Brazen serpent as the symbol of the higher side of mind with its knowledge and wisdom that could cure all the malaise of the lower mind.

The worship of the Brazen serpent with God's patronage continued till the time of Hezekiah who failed to see the wisdom of Moses and who contemptuously destroyed it describing it as a piece of brass. But Hezekiah did not succeed in destroying the symbol from the people's mind. We see years later. St John the Divine speaking about it in the following lines:

> "And as Moses lifted up the serpent in the wilderness,
> even so must the son of man be lifted up."

In Biblical accounts the serpents are not represented as evil creatures. It was God's hand that formed them. One of the fallen angels assumed the form of a serpent to induce confidence in Eve and worked havoc for humanity by inducing her (Eve) the mother of humanity, to eat the fruit of the forbidden tree.

It may be noted that the serpent did not do any harm to mother (Avvai). It was the Satan in the garb of the serpent who did the harm. The serpents of the Bible are to be considered only as symbol of mental qualities which could produce both good and evil. Jesus Christ scolded the

pharisees as "Ye Serpents, the generation of vipers, how can ye escape the damnation of hell". They should not be identified with Satan nicknamed as 'Old Serpent', the destructive principle of life. "Do evil" is the devil. Ill done to Eve is the evil and the doer of this evil has become the devil.

The head of the elephant and the inveiglement of the serpent in an integrated form appear to be a phase in the evolution of the figure of Ganesha as is seen in the piece of sculptures containing the figure of a man with the head of an elephant holding among other features, the tail of a serpent, preserved in Paris Museum.

Ganesha has yet to acquire his mount the mouse.

GANESHA AND HIS MOUNT

The little mouse which is seen as the mount of Ganesha is the most enigmatic figure in his image or picture. Just as the English word cow a domestic animal which gives milk got mixed up with the sanskrit mystic word 'Gao' the word mouse in English also got mixed up with another sanskrit word Mushika which is explained in some detail in Chapter ten.

The mouse which lives in its burrow throughout the day shunning sunlight was associated in ancient Egypt with all mystic rites. It was in spite of its apathy for sunlight dedicated to Horus the Sun God and was considered as an external manifestation of the soul which lives inside the body. It was kept in temples as a sacred animal and when it died its body was mummified and preserved. Herodotus says that in the Temple of Hephaestus in Egypt there is a statue of an Egyptian King with a mouse in his hand with the words "Look on me for the Gods." In some Ganesha temples in India also even at the present time mice are kept and fed with milk and sweet meat and they move about without fear. From Egypt the cult appears to have spread to Greece and Rome where also mice were held as sacred animals, fed and kept in temple and other religious sanctuaries.

In the Old Testament of the Bible there is the reference of a trespass offer of five Golden mice by the Philistines, a non-semitic race, to the Israelites for the wrongful detention of their Ark containing the sacred rolls. The trespass offer is an illustration of the usage of Golden mice having the colour of pure gold for expiatory purposes. Pure gold is called in India as 'Musa gold'. The crucible used for melting gold is called muz. The burrow where the golden mouse lives is also called muz and that is why it is called in Sanskrit "Mushikam', a word derived from Muz which got into the English vocabulary as mouse. Mice like serpents are shunned as loathsome creatures. But like serpents they attained considerable mystic significance. It is in keeping with this, a tiny mouse is seen carrying the heavy weight of Ganesha.

It may be noted that the golden mouse is the smallest mammal in whom the relationship of the mother and child is more apparent. Elephant is the biggest among the land mammals and man occupies the top most position between these two mammals from the point of view of this physical and mental evolution. It may be noted that the human part of the form in Ganesha image is in between his elephant head and the mouse, his mount. There is no doubt that there is a meaningful and mystic design for the mouse to come into the figure of Ganesha with an elephant head on a human body. We have to decipher the design and the meaning behind it.

In the Thaithiriya Brahmana there is a reference about a feud between GOD Agni (Fire) and other Gods. Agni disappeared into the earth assuming the form of a mouse. Later on when there was a truce among the parties, this mouse by common consent was presented to Shiva. Shiva energised by the possession of this mouse generated Karthikeya popularly known as Subramanya in South India. After the generation of Karthikeya Shiva made a present of the mouse to his elder son, Ganesha, who was for a long time without a mount as could be seen in the early Gupta period works of art.

The reference in the Thaithiriya Brahmana that Agni disappeared into the earth assuming the form of a mouse is very significant. Agni in Vedic literature according to Aurobindo is indicative of "Truth conscious seer - will", "Divine energism" and the "force of Rudra", Agni is also one of the Vedic Gods.

"Indrum, Mitram Varunam Agnim ahuratho divyah Suparno Garuthman Ekam sat Vipra bahudha vadantha. Agnim Yamam Matarisvanam ahu" (They called him Indra Mitra, Varunam Agni and he is heavenly noble winged bird the sun; to what is one of Rishis gave various names. They called him Agni, Yama Matariswanam).

 Agni, which became the mount of Ganesha assuming the form of mouse is also mentioned as one of the twentyfive principles on which the sankya system is built. Sankya is purely a psychic system and these twentyfive principles are beyond the scope of ordinary cognition.

The first principle is Prakrithi which is the uncaused primordial undifferentiated matter.

The second is the Mahat the subtle cosmic substance (The cosmic intelligence).

The third is the Ahankara (the ego) which is acted upon by the three strands of quality, the Sathva, Rajas and Thamas in Prakrithi. From Ahankara came out four different groups of principles each group containing five sub principles as detailed below:

I.	Tan Mathras	1.	Sabda	(sound)
		2.	Sparsa	(touch-feeling)
		3.	Rupa	(form)
		4.	Rasa	(taste)
		5.	Gandha	(smell)
II.	Gnanendrias	1.	Shrotra	(ear)
		2.	Twak	(skin)
		3.	Chaksha	(eyes)
		4.	Rasa	(tongue)
		5.	Gharana	(nose)

III.	Karmendrias		1.	Vak	(mouth)
			2.	Pani	(hand)
			3.	Padam	(leg)
			4.	Payur	(anus)
			5.	Upastham	(genitals)

(please see separate commentaries in Chapter 8).

IV.	Maha Buthas		1.	Akasa	(ether)
			2.	Vayu	(air)
			3.	Agni	(fire)
			4.	Aup	(water)
			5.	Prithvi	(earth)

On an analysis of the Prithvi (earth) thatwa (principle) of the Maha Buthas, it can be seen that it contains the essence of all the five Tanmathras. The following table will make it clear:

TABLE

$$(1)\quad \frac{\text{Akasa}}{\text{Ether}} - \frac{\text{Sabda}}{\text{Sound}}$$

$$(2)\quad \frac{\text{Vayu}}{\text{Air}} - \frac{\text{Sabda}}{\text{Sound}} + \frac{\text{Sparsa}}{\text{Touch}}$$

$$(3)\quad \frac{\text{Agni}}{\text{Fire}} - \frac{\text{Sabda}}{\text{Sound}} + \frac{\text{Sparsa}}{\text{Touch}} + \frac{\text{Rupa}}{\text{Form}}$$

$$(4)\quad \frac{\text{Ap}}{\text{Water}} - \frac{\text{Sabda}}{\text{Sound}} - \frac{\text{Sparsa}}{\text{Touch}} + \frac{\text{Rupa}}{\text{Form}} + \frac{\text{Rasa}}{\text{Taste}}$$

$$(5)\quad \frac{\text{Prithvi}}{\text{Earth}} - \frac{\text{Sabda}}{\text{Sound}} + \frac{\text{Sparsa}}{\text{Touch}} + \frac{\text{Rupa}}{\text{Form}} + \frac{\text{Rasa}}{\text{Taste}} + \frac{\text{Gandha}}{\text{Smell}}$$

The above table will show that Agni which contains elements of sound, touch and form occupies the middle position between Akasa and Vayu on the one side and water and earth on the other side. These sides may be termed as higher and lower sides.

So far we have accounted for twenty three principles of the Sankya system. The remaining two principles are Manas (Mind) and Purusha, the spirit.

The metamorphosis of Agni into a mouse and its getting into the earth and subsequent capture and presentation to Shiva is an allegory of a mystical nature,

....15

signifying the role of Agni in spiritual matters symbolised as a mouse in the set up of Ganesha.

Agni is the energising factor of life which Prometheus got from Olympus for the use of man even according to Greek mythology. When the energising factor leaves, the body becomes cold and dead. It appears from masonic legends and other sources that religious consecration or baptism among the ancient communities was by fire. Even the name of free mason is derived from the old name of pyre messon meaning children of fire. The fire walking ceremony prevalent among the Saiva sect of Hindus and among certain Muslim sects even at the present time is a relic of this ancient custom signifying the holiness of fire. God gave darsan to Moses in the form of fire and it was again God as Jothir Lingam, a pillar of fire that guided the Israelites during the night time in their exodus from Egypt. Since Agni, the energising power lies dormant in all forms of existence, it is compared to the golden mouse which lies hidden in its burrow unseen by anybody. In the light of this exposition and what is written further in Chapter 10, the importance of mouse as the vehicle of Ganesha should be appreciated.

Ganesha with his vehicle now gets a mystic power which is recognised by both the ritualism of Vedas and the mysticism of yoga and this makes him a Deity of no mean importance.

We have yet to consider him vis-a-vis Shiva, his reputed parent, the great Lord of Yoga.

From the Art Gallery

Green Marble Ganesha from Bhubaneshwar, Orissa

GANESHA AND SHIVA

*B*rahma, Vishnu and Shiva are the three mighty Gods forming the Hindu Trinity. Of these Brahma and Vishnu are mentioned in Vedas. There is no mention of Shiva. But there is the mention of a Deity by name Rudra to whom prayers are addressed for saving men from the effects of lightening and for protecting the sacrificial fire. He was considered as a mighty violent Deity having power over fire (Agni) living in Himalayan heights among the clouds.

Although Rudra was a mighty God he was not on a par with Indra, the Deity in Chief of the Aryans. Obviously, Shiva did not find a place in the early Vedic literature as he was a non Aryan God belonging to a different cult. He was recognised only at a later period as one of the Gods in the Vedic literature along side of Rudra. We find this in the Kaivalyopanishad. "Sa Brahma, Sa Vishnu, Sa Shiva Sokshara" (He is Brahma, He is Vishnu, He is Rudra, he is Shiva and he is indestructible). Evidently when this upanishad came into being the merger of Rudra with Shiva had not taken place.

In the seals of the ancient Indus Valley there are figures of yogis and these may be correctly surmised to be representations of Shiva. There is however no seal where, in any, figure, he is seen riding a bull. Even in the seal depicting the Yogi surrounded by animals, the lion and the bull are conspicuous by their absence. Perhaps the Lord of Yoga got his consort riding a lion and his own mount the bull only at a later date.

Yoga is a prevedic cult with a personal inner approach to solve the spiritual problems of life. This is different from the Vedic Cult of Yoga with either a collective or individual and even a vicarious approach of overt ritualism hoping to solve the same problems. In Yaga, there is recital of Mantras. In Yoga, there is only Ajapa (non-recital) contemplation. Yoga is a Dravidian Cult. But it is believed by some scholars that Shiva, the Lord of Yoga, was propitiated by the worship of his idol or his symbol, the Linga, and it was the Dravidian who introduced Idol worship. This belief is inconsistent with the ideal of Yoga. The Holy Cross is a Christian symbol. Any sanctity shown to this symbol will not amount to a worship of God which is as enjoined by Christian doctrine, to be in spirit and in truth. Bible in the genesis chapter mentions that Jacob set up a pillar as a symbol of God's house and poured oil on it. Any respect shown to this pillar will not amount to the worship of Jehovah. Similarly the pillars (lingas) and the imaginary figure of Shiva personified as a yogi excavated from the Indus Valley should be considered only as religious symbols. Any sanctity shown to these symbols and images is neither worship of Shiva nor the practice of Yoga. The meaning of Shiva Linga has to be understood in the light of the revelation of St. John "Him that overcometh will I make a pillar in the temple of my God and he shall go no more out." It may be noted that Shiva is called Sthanu, a word derived from thoon meaning pillar, in Dravidian Tamil.

It may be noted that Thera, the father of Abraham was a manufactures of idols and linga pillars and Abraham, the grand-father of Jacob, was worshipping a God by name El-Shaddai, a mountain-God along with his symbol, the linga pillar. El-Shaddai looks like another name for Shiva, the God of Mount Kailas known among his original Dravidian devotees as Shaddayan and Shaddayappan. Shaddam or jaddam means body or basic matter and the names El-Shaddai, Shaddyan and Shaddayappan mean, the God who energises the body or basic matter with life. Abraham is said to have consecrated a grove (Pillar) at Beer-she-Ba in honour of his God before he crossed over to Egypt. The worship of El-Shaddai continued until the name was replaced by Moses by the name of 'Y H W·H' rendered in English as Jehovah.

The practice of yoga with its moral and mental discipline appealed to the psychic sense of the Aryan invaders who had settled down in the Indus Valley. Yoga was considered to be superior to Yaga. This opinion was endorsed by Adi Shankara who said that the Valley rites are for those who are in the grip of desires.

These two cults did not remain long as irreconcilable being based on two different doctrines. By a process of interpreting vedic terms and expressions the masters of vedanta synthesised them under a yoga-cum-bakthi oriented philosophy which today goes by the name of Hindu culture and which however is different from popular Hinduism. With this synthesis the concept of Shiva as the benevolent and merciful God manifesting as the principle of life, received a separate identity. The mighty God of fire, Rudra, did not maintain his vedic individuality for long. He got merged with Shiva and his several names also became synonymous with the several names of Shiva.

Shiva the lord of Yoga is said to be residing on Mount Kailas lying to the North of Indus Valley. He is in this sense very much like the Olympian God. The sanctuary of Shiva as Mount Kailas is very meaningful. Kailas is a word of Dravidian Origin. 'Ka' means 'head' and 'vilas' means 'residence'. Kailas is a corruption of the compound word, Ka-vilas, meaning the residence which is 'Head' or the residence of Jeeva (the life principle) inside the brain in the 'Head'. Jeeva in course of time became identical with Shiva meaning the same life principle. If Shiva leaves the body, the body becomes Shava (dead). Sufis call Shiva 'the Hyat' and the Shava 'the Mayat'. The Worship of God as Shiva was prevalent in Arabia before the advent of Islam. It is said that the uncle of the Prophet of Islam, Umar-Bin-e-Hassham, was an ardent devotee of Shiva and he is said to have laid down his life for his faith.

The son of God conception is not foreign to Hinduism. Hindu mythology credits Shiva with two sons. The elder one is Ganesha, the younger one is

Karthikeya. There is however some difference in the mode of their genesis. Ganesha is the creation of Parvathy without participation of her consort Shiva and Karthikeya is the creation of Shiva without the participation of Parvathy. But both Shiva and Parvathy own their percentage notwithstanding their peculiar and separate immaculate origin.

Ganesha's origin through his mother, obviously is a reference to the prevedic matriarchal society where he was already a Deity along with female Deities under the overall supremacy of his mother Parvathy, known as Ambal, the Magna Mater of the Univese. Shiva enjoyed the status of a consort and nothing more, before her. But he was the lord of Yoga. As the lord of yoga, he had a good following. During the vedic period his followers were seen having long hair and because of this they were called Kesins. They did not follow vedic rites. They wandered about as Saiva ascetics carrying waterpots in their hands. These wandering mendicants were known as vratyas (one who renounced vratas or rites). As they attained many mystic powers, by their meditative practice they were feared and avoided by the vedic priests like poisonous snakes. The reference of the great serpent Vratra who intercepted waters and light of the vedic priests may be a reference to these in the vedic literature. Karthikeya the Second son of Shiva did not attain the stature of Ganesha in the Hindu Pantheon. When upanishads came to be written about fifteen of them were devoted to the lord of Kailas. One Upanishad by name Ganpathyopanishad was exclusively devoted to Ganesha. Till then he had a mixed reception. Even Manu referred him only as a Deity of the Sudras. "Vinayaka Shudra Devatha". This reference about him clearly indicates that he was not acceptable to Brahmin Communities who performed yaga or sacrificial ceremonies. Ganapathyopanishad placed Ganesha on a par with Shiva and he was also considered as a tutelary Deity of Yoga.

Adi Shankara the expounder of non-dualism (Adwaitha) who was himself a great yogi, in his wisdom and consideration for ordinary people belonging to all communities countenanced panchayatana worship of five Deities which included Ganesha, the other Deities being Shiva, Sura (Sun), Vishnu and Ambal. Obviously Shankara thought such devotional form of worship may help a devotee to merge his mind in the Deity which symbolically is ending the state of duality. If the devotion is tainted then, the merger will amount to a delusion brought about by something like self hypnotism. If the devotion is pure then the devotee imperceptibly comes into the path of yoga. Shankara also had made it clear that the Panchayatana Deities are essentially one and the same though they appear differently to the uninitiated.

Although Ganesha images appear to be jumbles of incongruent parts, Shankara considered the images as meaningful symbols. He had described the meaning in the following lines in his "Ganesha Bhujangam".

"Ya mekaksharam nirmalam nirvikalpam gunathithamanda

makara sunyam" which means — The one imperishable, stainless, unconditioned, transcending qualities, supreme bliss and formless.

Ganesha also attracted the Tamil Saint and Poetess Avvayar who wrote her Akaval explaining how Ganesha is a symbol of all knowledge about yoga and how his devotees will be benefited by his worship knowing the full implications of what he stands for.

To appreciate this yoga aspect of Ganesha, we have to know something about yoga.

GANESHA AND YOGA

*Y*oga is not worship; nor is it a sacrifice to propitiate a Deity. The word yoga comes from the root 'yug' which means to join. It is described in the Vishnu Purana as follows:

"Having controlled all senses with the mind, the idea of unity of the self, with the supreme self within, is yoga."

According to Bhagavath Githa, yoga is the mind getting merged with the soul within, freeing itself from all attachments that bring about pain. The yoga sutra says that it is restraint of mental modifications or control of thought waves in mind.

"Yogaschittavrithi Nirodha"

Mrs. Annie Besant says that it is a science by which alone spiritual truths can be fully realised by the gradual unfolding of the inner faculties, which enable man to study the invisible world directly by the expansion of his consciousness to embrace wider and subtler ranges of being.

The object of yoga is to get moksha, that is to say, to emancipate the individual self from its bondage to the material world by a process of mental and bodily discipline culminating in a spiritual transformation and merger of the self with the supreme self, the God within. This merger secures for the yogi the moksha which is freedom from re-birth the bugbear of all thinking Hindus and others who believe in re-birth.

Yoga is said to be a prevedic cult. This was systematised on a scientific basis by sage Kapila who lived about the 7th century B.C. This organised wisdom which influenced the buddhist thought a good deal came to be known as sankya yoga or sankya philosophy. About five centuries later sage Pathanjali popularised it by introducing certain steps-in-aid known as Ashtanga (eight limbs of aid). He also insisted that a fervent devotion of God should also be considered as an indispensable factor in the practice of yoga, although five centuries before him, Sage Kapila did not think so.

Pathanjali's yoga came to be known as Ashtanga yoga or Raja Yoga. After Pathanjali, especially after the advent of puranic Hinduism, several systems of yoga came into existence such as Hatha yoga, Gnana yoga, Bhakthi yoga, Karma Yoga, Kundalini Yoga, Kriya Yoga, the latest one being the internal yoga of the 20th century systematised by the sage of Pondichery, Aurobindo.

These several systems except the integral yoga came into existence as both sankya yoga and Pathanjali's yoga exacted too much of a mental and moral discipline from the sadhakas (students) of yoga. Moreover, there were differences in temperaments and talents among them and something had to be done to accommodate the different degrees of moral and mental capacities of these sadhakas (students), besides meeting the exigencies of social, cultural and religious needs and changes.

In the process of this accommodation many moral lapses and mental perversions have taken place, twisting and misinterpreting the ideology of the old yoga and introducing many abominable practices in utter disregard of all moral and ethical values. Mesmerism, hypnotism and magic paraded under the garb of yoga and many unscrupulous men are seen going about commercialising their capacity to make a living.

 The integral yoga of Aurobindo retains all the salient and ethical features of the old yoga system. But its main aim appears to be to divinise man and make the earth a paradise for him to live through the grace of the supramental force.

People often mistake yoga asanas, the various physical posture in the nature of physical exercise as the cult of yoga. These asanas constitute but one among the eight steps in aid in the practice of yoga. The most vital part in the practice of yoga is the moral discipline that includes truthfullness, chastity, non-violence, right conduct and right living. For the student of yoga it is a bold adventure of the spirit into the realms beyond the thought or imagination of the common man.

Taking Ashtanga yoga as the standard we have to understand the eight limbs or steps in aid of yoga. They are as follows:

(1) **Yama**: This is the initial step. The trainee (sadhaka) in yoga has to practice certain negative viruses like abstention from evil thinking and evil doing.

(2) **Niyama**: In this step the trainee has to develop and practice positive virtues and follow certain moral codes and standards of conduct.

(3) **Asana**: In this step the trainee has to improve his health and physical fitness. The body is the temple of God and also the vehicle of Karma. It is therefore the duty of every one to keep his body clean and fit. Asana comprises various postures of sitting and physical twists and bends which the trainee is expected to do every day with a view to keep his body in a healthy condition. Ill health and practice of yoga cannot go together.

Asana exercise is different from other forms of exercise like running, jumping, weight lifting and swimming where maximum energy is spent with minimum benefit. In the asana exercise there is not much scope for the play of ego and maximum benefit is obtained with minimum energy spent. Asana exercises stimulate glands and internal organs. They are capable of curing many bodily ailments which stand as impediments in the practice of yoga. The efficacy of Asana exercises is being recognised in the western countries and America for maintaining health and physical fitness.

(4) **Pranayama**: This is a step as the name indicates of storing prana or vital energy which is the pivot of the training in yoga. Prana is the life principle in motion as the Holy breath of life acting on the five sensory organs bringing out the impressions of the phenomenal world.

Sage Thiruvalluvar says in his 'Kural': "They gain the world who grasp and tell of taste, sight, hearing, touch and smell." The phenomenal world is a concomitance of these senses and is sustained by the lower side of the mind or ego of every individual. In course of time he becomes aware of that fact that his senses are gaining for him only ephemeral sensation and not lasting happiness. He finds himself a victim in the meshes of his own web or mental involvements and wants to extricate himself. The extrication, popularly known as Moksham, is possible only by undoing his own involvements with his own senses. In a very cryptic manner Bhagvan Satya Sai Baba has described Moksham as Moha Kshayam which means ending all desires.

Yama, Niyama and Asana are three preparatory steps to regulate the external sadhana (training) of the sadhaka (students). Pranayama is a transitory step to get on to other steps regulating the internal sadhana or exercise of the student of yoga.

(5) **Pratyahara**: With this step the inner training of the sadhaka begins. He practices the retracting of the sense organs from the objects of senses.

(6) **Dharana**: This is the practice of concentration. The trainee pins his thought on any noble or spiritual concept to gain control over his mind.

(7) **Dhayana**: This is the practice of meditation by the sadhaka fixing his attention to his mind centre located inside the middle of his brows. The great Buddhist monk Bodhi Dharma of Conjeevaram commended this practice and carried it to China where it came to be known as Chan. From China it spread to Korea and thence to Japan where it came to be known as Zen.

(8) **Samadhi**: This is the highest stage of ecstatic consciousness in the yoga practice. The trainee attains perfect stillness of thought in which the sense of individuality or ego is extinguished. At this stage the sadhaka is held to win various miraculous powers called Vibuthi. The sadhaka becomes a siddha or paramahamsa who is superior to an ascetic and even to men of knowledge and action, according to Bhagavat Githa.

It may be noted that the above mentioned exercises or steps in aid are not meant to be practiced one after another. As far as possible the sadhaka has to bring them into his daily routine of life without prejudice to his other responsibilities.

It may not be out of place here to mention that the moral basis of the Hindu way of life is based on the observance of all or any one or more of these steps irrespective of the fact whether one is a sadhaka or not. The first two steps in aid by themselves form a complete code of ethics of universal application and each step by itself is a piece of virtue which if followed properly would imperceptibly lift one up to higher levels of spiritual thoughts and insights.

In the path of yoga many go wrong in the practice of pranayama which is aimed at the control of breath preventing its misuse and waste. Breathing is the symbol of life and stands first among the bodily functions of Prana manifested through the sense organs of the body. That is why in the practice of yoga the first thing to be tackled is the breath. Breath of life is directly connected with the psyche. For this reason Pranayam should be practised correctly as otherwise it will cause great harm to the health of the trainee. Any amount of book reading will not help. The trainee should approach it with great moral preparation. He should be initiated by a master who is an adept.

The practice of Pranayama roughly consists of neutralising the incoming and outgoing breaths called prana and apana without causing any restraint or strain in the normal manifestation of life in the form of breath. Apana should be taken as that which is not Prana (Apana). This neutralisation can be effected only inside the breathing apparatus, at the throat level below the base of brain stimulating medulla, pituitary and pineal regions of the brain. This is hinted in Bhagavat Githa Ch. V 27-29, where it is stated that the sadhaka (trainee) should sit tranquil concentrating his attention at the middle point of the brow neutralising Prana and Apana.

Katopanishad describes prana as the upward movement of the breath and Apana as its downward movement "urdham prana munna yathyapanam prathy a gasathy." Many do pranayam by alternate closing of one of the nostrils with the finger and retaining the breath as long as possible. This is not the correct method, as no neutralisation is effected in this practice. The writer has been warned against this practice by his Guru Swami Sivananda Parama Hamsa, the founder of Siddha Samaj who is now in Nirvikalpa Samadhi. He has also pointed out to the writer the common mistake that people make in the practice of yoga, which is beyond caste, colour, creed or sex and the wrong notions they have imbibed regarding certain vital terms and expressions used in the yoga literature. The writer is only a student of yoga. But he feels constrained that he should, with humility, share the knowledge he has gained with the readers for their benefit.

The initial mistake that is often made, is with regard to the understanding of the

श्री हरिद्रा गणेश सिद्धी यन्त्र

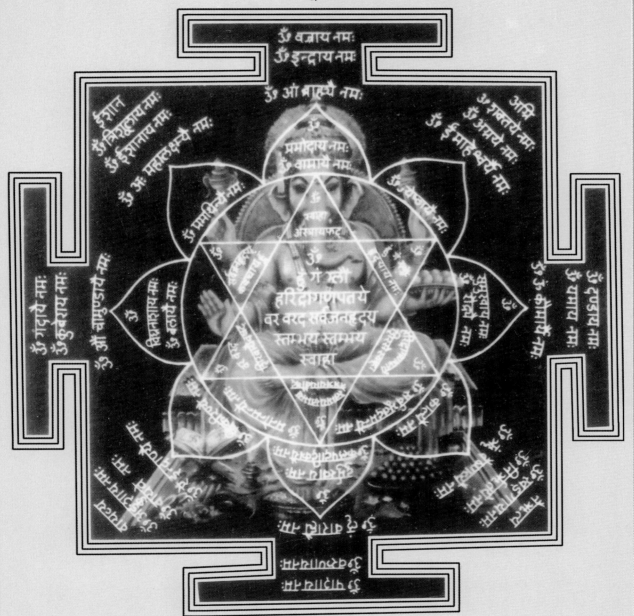

ॐ गं गणपतये नमः

पाशाङ्कुशौ मोदकमेकदन्तं करैर्दधानं कनकासनस्थम् ।
हारिद्रखण्डप्रतिमं त्रिनेत्रं पीतांशुकं रात्रिगणेशमीडे ॥

Papier Mache Ganesha from Pattur village in Andhra Pradesh

three Kalas or Nadies, viz. Ida, Pingala and Sushumna. Yoga being a prevedic cult one has to trace the prevedic origin of the terms usually employed in the yoga literature, from their Dravidian or proto Dravidian sources. Kala is the Shakti or energy, inherent in jeeva the life principle. It is the creative force from which impulses of creation start in the form of monadic Bindu which vibrates as Nada. From Nada the phenomenal world evolves. Kala is called Nadi (that which is moving) because of the flow of Nada. As Nada is the immediate cause of the phenomenal world it is called Nada Brahman, and Shakthi, its original source is called Nada Rupa (form of sound).

Ida Nadi is wrongly understood as the flow of air through the left nostril starting from the anus region and Pingala as the flow of air through the right nostril, also starting from the anus region. Sushumna is considered to be some current or energy also starting from the anus region and plying in between Ida Nadi and Pingala Nadi. It is because of this wrong notion that the practice of pranayam is wrongly done by many by closing the right and left nostrils alternately and performing the breathing process, retaining the breath inside the lungs by force, as long as possible.

Pranayam is an exercise with the Holy breath of life, leading to Prathyahara, Dharana, Dhyaa and finally to Samadhi. The right nostril does not take air only to the right lung. It takes air to the left lung also. Similarly, the left nostril serves both the lungs. Even granting that Ida Nadi and Pingala Nadi are the flow of breath through the left and right nostrils, how could one do pranayam if one is born without hands or the hands become incapacitated or the nose itself is destroyed by disease or some other mishap. Yoga is a path of mental discipline for the spiritual purpose of emancipating humanity from a life of strife and sorrow. Hence this path should be universal in its scope and application, and not be considered as the monopoly of a few fortunate individuals.

Every day when we sleep, without our knowing it, we relapse into a yoga like experience, having withdrawn our mind from the material world. At this time the mind touches the fringes of the inner reality provided the sleep is absolutely sound. This inner reality is the cosmic reservoir of energy — the Manasarovar and that is the reason why we feel fresh and vigorous when we wake up. In sound sleep there is complete black out of the world and there is no closing of the right or left nostril involved.

There is however a difference between yoga like experience in deep sleep and the actual experience in samadhi; according to my master and others who have realised the state of samadhi, the yoga is a sleep without sleeping where the mind loses its identity having merged itself with the inner reality. In deep sleep the mind retains its identity. It has only withdrawn itself from the objects of senses and the sleep itself should be considered as an internal wave of thought about nothingness.

Bhagavan Sathya Sai Baba clarifies that the difference between deep sleep and Samadhi is that in Samadhi the happiness is known at the time it occurs.

The description of the three Nadies Ida, Pingala and Sushumna as found in the yoga literature is as follows:

"Ida Bagirathi Prokta
Pingala Yamunayacha
Thayor Madhaye gatham Nadi
Sushumnakyam Saraswati."

Ida is said to be the flow of Bagirathi (Ganga). Pingala is the flow of Yamuna. The Nadi which flows through the middle of the brow is Saraswathi. In the above quoted verses the three Nadies are symbolised as three psychic rivers, viz. Ganga, Yamuna and Saraswathi. These rivers should not be confounded with terrestrial rivers of the same names. Some knowledge about these three psychic rivers will be useful in the understanding and the practice of yoga.

Hatha Yoga describes Ida as moon, the symbol of the mind and Pingala as Sun, Symbol of soul (Atman). The moon has no light of its own. It has to depend on Sun for its light. In the same manner the mind has no light of its own apart from what it gets from the soul or life principle within. Idom in Dravidian means, a place, a spot and may even mean the wide space. This word Idom is derived from Ida which is the Kala that has brought about the phenomenal world which is also called by the name of Bhaga. Ratham means flow. So Bhagiratham means the flow of phenomenal world from its causal point the jeeva or life principle. This flow is symbolised as Ganges (Ganga) flowing down to earth from the head of Shiva. The legendary account of king Bagiratha bringing down the Ganges from Akasa (heavens) in the Devi Bhagavatham should be understood in this light, to make the legend a purposeful study. Ida is to be understood as the creative force which made the world apparent to the senses and not as the flow of breath through the left nostril.

The word Pingala is misunderstood as the flow of breath through the right nostril. Pingala is also a word of Dravidian origin, 'Pin' means rearward. 'Kala' comes from the root 'Kal' meaning Air. So Kala means the force of air or the force of life energy. Pinkalai therefore is indicative of the receding or retracting force that withdraws the mind towards sushumna or seat of soul. Pingala is only a corruption of the word Pinkalai. It is also significant that the Sun which is symbol of the soul is also known by the name Pingala. Amarakosa mentions Yamuna as Surya Thanaya (daughter of Sun) which is also significant. In mystic, language, Ida the outgoing force is symbolised by sound symbol 'Ham' and the incoming force by sound symbol 'Sam'. Both put together becomes 'Hamsam' the cosmic swam the vehicle of Brahma the creator, a very meaningful expression.

Sushumna is another Nadi which is also misunderstood as rising from the anus region and proceeding up along the spine to the Brahma's seat inside the head.

This Nadi is also called Saraswathi. Sushumna is known in Dravidian as Chuzhimunai which means the whorl point or the point of coiled energy. The word Saraswathi is a mystic word with two concepts viz. Saram meaning the breath of life and Swathi or jothi meaning light. Saraswathi therefore means the seat of Divine Light from which breath of life emanates. In Tamil there is a saying "Saram Parpon Param Parka Koodum" meaning 'He who takes care of his breath will be able to attain the Infinite'. Saraswathi is described as an underground river. This is indicative of the fact that the Sushumna Nadi functions inside the brain and could be located as the source of the Holy Breath of life. Saraswathi is also personified as a Goddess carrying a Veena (musical instrument). The Veena in her hand is a symbol of Nada Brahmam or the creative force. It should be noted that Sushumna is a physic force in man of supreme importance and Ida and Pingala are only its two aspects. They are not three separate forces which function along side of the spine.

The realisation of Saraswathi is through Saranagathi. Saranagathi is a contraction of Sara-Vana-Gathi. Sara meaning the breath of life, Vana meaning the light and Gathi meaning path. This is the Savya path of light extolled by sages, the path of Pranayam or the path of yoga to become one with God.

Speaking about Saraswathi, Bhagavan Sathya Sai Baba has expounded that she has for her carrier the Hamsa or the Breath of Life, the stoppage of which would mean the disappearance of Saraswathi who is regarded as one that could lead us from death to immortality. The prayer 'Mrithyorma amritham Gamaya' meaning 'from death lead me to immortality' is an invocation to her so that the jeevi, the embodied soul, may escape the thraldom of rebirth. It may be noted that Sharada meaning that which moves Saram is another name for Saraswathi meaning the Saram that is light, based on the core word saram denoting the holy breath of life the moving symbol of God in all living beings.

 Bhagavan also discloses the real significance of Saranagathi an expression co-related to Sarm which is understood as absolute surrender to God. He says that it is only when we feel that the Divine is present in all human beings, and in other living things and that this Divinity is omnipresent can we understand the real meaning of Saranagathi which is surrender in thought, word and deed to God, so as to become one with Him. This is self realisation.

Yoga is not a monopoly of the Hindus. It is said that the Essenes community of the Jews practised and lived a life of Yoga and Jesus Christ was born in this community. In the Old Testament of the Bible the worship of God appears to have been done by sacrifice similar to Yaga practice by the vedic Aryans. Jesus Christ reformed this mode of worship into one of prayer by Ajapa (without utterance). He taught that the kingdom of god is within and that god being a spirit should be worshipped in spirit. He instructed his disciples that they should have an inner approach when they pray. He said, "when thou prayest enter into thy closet and when hast shut thy door pray to thy father which is in secret."

The door meant here is the mental door and not the closet door. This is a yogic approach. "Commune with your own heart upon your bed and be still" is what the Psalmist in the Bible says. The muslim sufis also practiced yoga under the name of saluk. They called pranayam, Habs-e-Dam. In his Mathnavi Maulana Rumi says "close your eyes, your lips and your ears and if you fail to discover the secrets of god, laugh at me."

Before this chapter is closed it has to be mentioned that the realisation of the Eight Siddhies or psychic powers by the practice of yoga is not the end and aim of life. The Siddhis should bring about self realisation by the annihilation of the ego as otherwise we have to be born again to suffer the results of our past actions. Our earthly existence is in the nature of an open air imprisonment with fretting and fuming. Our aim should be to see that we do not come back. In the story of Ramayana, we come across Ravana, the King of Lanka, having the eight siddhis. But he has not realised his self by the suppression of his ego. He went in for another man's wife and that was his disaster. We are seeing many such Ravanas going about the world even at the present time hoodwinking the world. One should be wary about accepting such men as Gurus or Preceptors.

Yoga is beyond barriers of race or religion and it can be the only unifying force to bring humanity together. But one should be careful about charlatans who make business out of it.

Yoga literature also spoke of six psychic centres which are also not properly understood. A correct understanding of these six centres is necessary to understand the science of yoga and to appreciate Ganesha's connection with it.

GANESHA AND PSYCHIC CENTRES

There are six psychic centres known as shadadharam in yoga language. 'Shad' means six. 'Adharam' means support. These supporting centres are:

(1)   Muladharam — said to be situated at the anus.

(2)   Swathishtanam — said to be situated at the genitals.

(3) Manipuram — said to be situated at the stomach.

(4) Anahatham — said to be situated at the heart.

(5) Visudhi — said to be situated at the throat.

(6) Ajna — said to be situated between the eye brows.

The location of these centres at the places above named is open to serious objections. We shall consider these centres one by one with reference to objections concerning them.

(1) **Muladharam:** This centre is said to be at the anus where Kundalini sakti the coiled energy or serpent energy is understood to be lying. This centre is also said to be presided over by the Ganesha. If this understanding is correct, then the proper places to install the images of Ganesha should be latrines and lavatories. Evidently, the correct location of Muladharam has not been properly understood. Mulam means cause or root. Adharam means the basic support, root cause of all human activities. We have to search for this spring and source only in the head and not anywhere else. In Dravidian the brain inside the head is called Moolai and this is a clue to fix the Muladharam at the proper place inside the head. In the Bhagavath Githa and Katopanishad there are references of a cosmic tree with roots up and branches down. Sufism teaches that the trees of paradise have their roots above. These metaphors are other clues or pointers to fix the muladharam inside the head.

Moreover, Muladharam is the centre where the Kundalini Sakti lies. The great Siddha Goraknath says about the location of Kundalini in his Gorakh Sathaka as follows:

"Kantordhavam kundalisaktirasthitha kundalakrithi,
Brahmadwara mukham nithyam mukhenachadya thishtathi."

which means that Kundalini Sakti lies above the throat and remains there covering the door of Brahma with her face. This will settle the question and the finding that Muladharam is not at the anus but at the head above the throat should be accepted.

The head as every one knows contains the brain covered by the skull. The brain contains three distinct portions, viz. (1) the Cerebrum (2) the Cerebellum (3) the Medulla Oblongata. The cerebellum is divided into two halves, the right and the left. The right half controls the left side of the body and the left half controls the right side of the body. This fact will expose the absurdity of identifying the flow of breath in the left nostril with Ida Nadi and flow of breath in the right nostril with Pingala Nadi. Besides its manifold functions it is the seat of memory and consciousness covering all evolutionary stages of existence of this life as also of the past. The cerebellum is situated under the hind part of the cerebrum. This portion of the brain regulates the equilibrium of the body and co-ordinate mental and physical activities.

The Medulla Oblongata is the smallest portion of the brain controlling the vital functions of the body such as regulation of heart beat and breathing. It also controls reflex centres and is situated just below the cerebellum. It is in fact a spinal bulge at the top of the neck. The spinal cord descending from this bulge through the vertebral column is only in the nature of a telegraph wire to carry impulses to and from brain and other parts of the body. If any part of the body is to be called Muladharam it should be this portion, the base of the brain. (See sketch No.1)

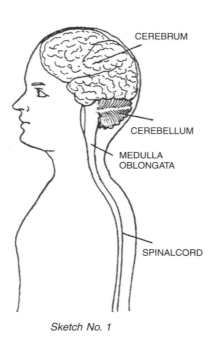

Sketch No. 1

The Medulla Oblongata, the neck and throat region of the body is called Kaluthu in Dravidian Tamil and Kantam in Aryan Sanskrit. The sacred syllable of Ganesha the presiding Deity of Muladharam is "Glowm or Gam." This sacred syllable as well as the anatomical terms like gullet and glottis and the sanskrit word galam for the neck are related to the Tamil word Kaluthu above which muladharam is situated. The above delineation would amply confirm the identity of Muladharam with Medulla Oblongata.

Ganesha the presiding Deity of Muladharam is also called Ganapathy meaning Lord of Hosts. There is some confusion in this name. During vedic period Ganapathy meaning lord of hosts was a title. This title was adopted by Indra and later by Shiva and even by Karthikeya. Ganapathy is a corruption of Kanapathy. Ganesha being a deity of prevedic period was considered to be the lord Kana as distinct from Gana meaning lord of hosts. Kana in Dravidian means sound (Nada). The Lord of Nada was called either by the name Kanesha (Kanam meaning Nada and Esan meaning 'Lord') or Kapapathy (Kanam meaning Nada and Pathy meaning Lord). Even in Sanskrit Kwana means sound produced by the musical instrument veena. When Ganesha became an important deity he appropriated the title of Ganapathy meaning lord of hosts for himself and the name Ganapathy was also added to the list of his several other names. The name Ganesha meaning lord of Nada is very appropriate for the reason that Nada (sound) is produced from the throat region controlled by Medulla Oblongata, which may be confirmed as muladharam of which Ganesha is the presiding deity.

Ganesha is also called by another name Vinayaka. Vinayaka really means lord of breath. "Vi' means air, 'Nayaka' means lord. The air meant here is the breath of life regulated by the Medulla Oblongata. Some interpret this name to mean one born without a sire, basing the interpretation on the puranic story that Ganesha came into existence as the mind born son of Parvathi. Ganesha being the presiding Deity of Muladharam the interpretation based on the science of yoga that he is the Lord of breath may be considered as more appropriate.

Regarding muladharam it is ungainly that this great psychic centre is considered to be situated at the anus region. Perhaps this wrong notion gained ground owing to misinterpretation arrived at by interpreters with meagre knowledge, taking the bottom end of the spinal column instead of the top end as Muladharam.

It may be noted that caduceus popularly known as the staff of Mercury, the messenger of gods is a symbol of the flow of Kundalini Sakti from the muladharam below Cerebellum. The eagle with spread wings mounted on the staff is the symbol of the Sun — the Atma. The heads of the two serpents entwining the staff appear just below the wings of the eagle drawing their energy from them. These serpents are positive and negative forces which by their interaction and flow down cause the appearance of the phenomenal world. It may not be correct to interpret that these serpents are hibernating in the anus region of the human system called muladharam, by mistake.

(2) **Swathisthanam:** This centre is said to be situated at the genitals. This is absurd. Swathi means light. Sthanam means place, position, region, locality, etc. This is the stage when the sadhaka gets a glimpse of the rays emanating from the Divine light situated far ahead within himself. He has to make further progress towards it. At the genitals, there is no light and it is not possible to generate any light there. At best one could generate some heat to produce a libido.

(3) **Manipuram:** This centre is said to be located at the stomach. The name Manipuram itself suggests that it is the City of the Sun which is the symbol of

the soul, the quest of the Sadhaka. It may be noted that this word soul is derived from the word 'sol' which means sun. Manipuram ad jyoti puram are the same referring to the Divine light within us. There is no Divine light in the stomach. A kick in the stomach produces pain, but not light, whereas a kick in the head produces both pain and flashes of

light. Sufis call this light as Huq Nur and Saivaits as Thiru Nir. According to the Aquarian Gospel of Jesus Christ Jesus is said to have told the Magians "You will see upon a living shrine, the candle of lord aflame and when you see it burning there, look deep within the temple of your brain and you will see it all aglow." As Jesus said, it is within the temple of our brain we have to search for this light and not at the stomach. It may be noted that organs below the diaphram help in the expression of grosser side of human nature while the organs above it, help in the expression of the spiritual side.

(4) **Anahatham**: This is said to be situated at the fleshy heart where there is only the sound of heart beat. Anahatham presupposes Ahatham. Music is of two kinds, viz. Ahatham and Anahatham. Ahatham is the music, produced by the mouth or by some other external modes. Anahatham is the unsung divine melodies heard inside the head. Plato called these Anahat melodies as the music of spheres.

The Sufis called this as the Kalam-i-Ilahi. In the yoga parlance it is the mellowed tone from the region of sushumna the neural heart divinised as Goddess Saraswathi. Her Veena is the symbol of this Anahat music. The lyre of Orpheus and the flute of Krishna are also similar symbols of Anahat music proceeding from the core of the heart. It is to this neural heart as distinguished from the fleshy heart that a reference is made in the Katopanishath as the seat of the soul.

"Angushta Mathra purusha antharatma sadha
jananam hridaye sannivistha."

(The inner soul called Purusha beams always in the heart of all persons embedded in a space small enough for the thumb tip.)

Evidently the mistake made by the interpreters was that they took the fleshy heart inside the thoracic cavity as the real heart instead of the neural heart inside the head embedded in the centre of the brain.

(5) **Visudhi**: This centre is said to be situated at the throat. This is not correct. 'Vi' means air; but not the atmospheric air. The air indicated here is the air represented by the Holy Breath of Life, an emanation from Chitakasa, the mind sky or knowledge space. Chit in essence is the mind stuff and Suddhi should be understood as the pure nature of the mind stuff. Vissudhi therefore should be understood as Chithasuddhi. 'Vi' should not be taken as a sound of negation in which case Vissudhi would mean impurity of mind. This is absurd.

(6) **Ajna**: This centre is said to be located between the eye brows and is generally understood to be the centre of command. This is a very superficial interpretation of the word Ajna. It should be noted that Ajna is the contracted form of Atmagnanam or knowledge about soul. After obtaining chitha suddhi, the sadhaka realises the Divinity in him and becomes

a superman. The legendary son of Ajana Devi by Vayu, she wind God, known as Anjaneya (Hanuman), the Monkey God of the Hindus is a symbol of a such a superman. Hanuman is also known as maruthi for the reason that he has control over his mind and the breath of life through which he has realised Ashta Sidhis (eight mystic powers.)

All the above mentioned centres from Muladhara to Ajna are stages in the spiritual development of the Sadhaka in his
quest to realise his self. This should not be taken as different tiers placed one over the other in the anatomy of the
sadhaka.

The present day concept of Ganesha is a synthesis of prevedic and vedic thoughts and his form is hieroglyphic in scope and design accommodating several cults of the Hindu religion. To the followers of Shiva, he is the son of Shiva, the lord of Yoga. To the followers of sakta cult, he is the son of Shakti, the Magna Mater. To the followers of Vishnu, he is an Alwar-cum-Deity, who could help them out of all their difficulties. To those who follow the path of yoga, he is a yoga murthy. The great Buddha is also known among the Hindus as Vinayaka, obviously for the reason that Buddha was an embodiment of the abstract conception of Ganesha as Vinayaka.

When yoga science and technique got mixed up with puranic love and ritualism people lost sight of the real significance of certain mystical terms and expressions connected with yoga and its practice. It is necessary that these mystical terms and expressions are properly understood to make this critical study of Ganesha purposeful. A few selected mystical terms are dealt with in the next chapter.

Shri Siddhivinayak – Siddhatek

GANESHA AND MYSTICAL TERMS

*I*n the chapter dealing with Ganesha and his mount we have noticed how Agni one of the twenty-five principles of the philosophy of Sankya became a mouse and how it was given to Ganesha who used it as his mount. As the Sankya system of thought formed the basis of all yoga systems in the subsequent periods we have to understand the correct import of these twenty-five principles. The Sankya philosophy is mainly metaphysical and psychological in its cope and any interpretation which is inconsistent with this scope is bound to mislead us. Among the twenty-five principles there is no difficulty in understanding twenty principles. But five, viz. (1) Vak said to be mouth, (2) Pani said to be hands (3) Padma said to be the legs (4) Payu said to be anus and (5) Upastham said to be the genitals are confusing. In the human body, the torso and the head are the most important parts. There are persons falling under the category of neutar gender. Obviously such persons cannot come under the category said to be envisaged by sankya. Moreover the mouth and anus are only two openings of one and the same organ the alimentary canal, the mouth being the opening into the organ and the anus being the opening out from the organ. The functions of these several organs are more physical than metaphysical, which the sankya system is.

The writer does not claim any wisdom in the correct understanding of these five terms apart from what he has learned from his master. The real meaning of these five terms may be taken as follows: Vak may be taken as the static reservoir of creative power within us; Pani as the torrential flow of Prana from this reservoir; Padam as the regulative force of Prana when in motion as the breath of life; Payu as the spreading of Prana to every part of the body and Upastham a compound word meaning one joined with another, as referring to Purusha in the grip of Prakrithi according to Thanthra cult of the later days. All these inner forces are subtle and the meaning of the words used to express them will become apparent only if we go into their physical and metaphysical background. Superficial meaning will mislead us. The word Karma in the expression Karmendria may also be understood, in the light of the above exposition, only as the Holy Breath of Life, which is always functioning without any stop, synonymous with the creative force that sustains the phenomenal world. For a fuller understanding of these metaphysical factors, we must examine the anatomy of the human body. No one can deny that all mental and physical activities are controlled by brain and certain brain organs. The activities envisaged by the six psychic centres and five karmendrias are really taking place within the ambit of space between the medulla oblongata and the region of the pineal gland inside the brain. In the samadhi stage all the psychic factors and indrias resolve themselves, into a single principle of potential voidness, a reservoir of infinite capacity or a positive Zero as Yogi Shuddhananda Bharathi calls it. (See Sketch No. 2)

Many are under the impression that the mind is situated in the fleshy heart inside the thoracic cavity. This is absurd and this absurdity is proved by the

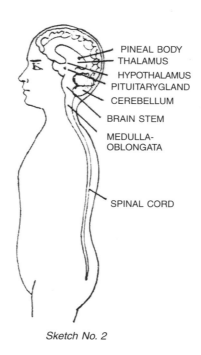

PINEAL BODY
THALAMUS
HYPOTHALAMUS
PITUITARYGLAND
CEREBELLUM

BRAIN STEM

MEDULLA-
OBLONGATA

SPINAL CORD

Sketch No. 2

transplantation of heart in human beings. The recipient of the new heart does not change his thoughts or character or bring any additional knowledge or traits of character or any special aptitude that the donor may have possessed. This shows that we must revise our old notions and ideas and the understanding of certain psychic terms used in yoga and other religious literature.

There are four expressions, viz. (1) the Linga, (2) the Yoni, (3) the Gutham (4) the Panchamakaram which are greatly misunderstood. This misunderstanding has taken people off the track of real knowledge. The lingam is understood as the phallus, the yoni as the female organ, the Gutham as anus and the Panchamakarm as eating gram, fish and flesh and indulging in wine and women. This perverted understanding of the above mentioned expressions is unfortunate. This perversion has brought into ridicule and contempt certain sections of the Hindu community. We have now to understand the correct meaning of these expressions.

Linga is the creative principle. Yoni is the matrix which energises the creative principles. Linga and Yoni are the male and female principles of life embedded in all its manifestations. Even in inanimate manifestations of matter, these principles can be traced as positive and negative forces.

Gutham is that which throws out 'Gao'. Gao is not cow; nor is it a cow Goddess. Harivamsa says that Gao stands for sound. Sage Aurobindo interprets Gao as light. Amarkosa says that the word indicates sound, light and earth. We may accept all these interpretations and declare that Gutham is not anus as popularly understood. Taking the meaning of the word gao as sound, the word gutham may approximate only with the voice box in the throat, with its reasoning spaces like sinuses nose, mouth, wind pipe and lungs, and not with rectum even by any stretch of imagination. Gutham is a sublime word. The title 'Gaothum' adopted by the great Rishis and also by Buddha is a pointer to the sublimity of this word. It is because of the lack of proper understanding of the psychic terms like these, people went wrong and degenerated themselves in eroticism of the Vama marga and other abominable practices and ceremonies.

Panchamakaram is another expression which is very much misunderstood. It is a secret mnemonic expression meant as a guide line for the worship of sakti (the supreme mother), in the course of the practice of yoga by the followers of the sakta cult. Panchamakaram denotes five steps in aid, the names of which begin with letter 'M' viz. (1) Mudra (2) Mathsyam (3) Mamsam (4) Madhyam (5) Maithunam. The real esoteric significance of these five words is as follows:

(1) **Mudra**: By Mudra is meant either Sambavi Mudra or Kesari Mudra.

Sambavi Mudra is performed according to the yoga sasthra in the following manner.

"Antarlakshyam Brahrdrishti
Nimishonmesha varjitha
Eshamsa sambavi Mudra
Sarvathanthrashu gopyatha".

The meaning of the above verse is that the sadhaka or worshipper should aim inwards with up turned eyes in a steady gaze obviously concentrating on the mind centre in the neural heart. This discipline is the underlying principle of all Thanthra forms of meditation.

Kesari Mudra is performed in the following manner according to Goraknath:

"Kapala kuhare jehwa
Pravishta viparithaga
Bruvoranthar gatha drishti
Mudra bavathi Kesari."

which means that the sadhaka or trainee should perform this mudra or discipline by turning the tongue over backwards into the hollow above the throat fixing his gaze between the eye brows.

(2) **Mathsyam**: Mathsyam means fish. Fish is a symbol of the mind. This fish is to be retrieved from the waters of Yamuna and Ganges and preserved in the reservoir of Saraswathi to obtain Divine knowledge and happiness. Hindu mythology speaks of god incarnating as a fish to save mankind and St. Augustian says that Jesus the son of God is a fish that lives in the midst of waters.

There is also a reference in the Holy Quran of a journey, by water undertaken by Moses in quest of knowledge to the confluence of two rivers. Half way Moses discovered that the fish which he brought for food had escaped in the river and he had to return to the starting point where he met a master who took him as a disciple. Prophet Mohamed taught spiritual truths in parables. The fish in the parable obviously is the mind which eluded the grasp of Moses.

(3) **Mamsam**: Mamsam means flesh which covers the bone frame work of the Temple in which god resides. This temple is verily our body Astinapur (City built of bones) where the forces of good live in juxtaposition with the forces of bad and where the forces of good ultimately overcome the forces of bad with the grace of God. The great Hindu epic 'Mahabharatha' is an allegory of the strife between good and bad forces within us wherein by the grace of God described as Krishna, the forces of good destroy the forces of bad. In the Epic, the City of Astinapur is delineated as Hastinapur. As fish is the symbol of the mind, flesh is the symbol of the body it has to be well preserved on the principle of a healthy mind in a healthy body. The flesh is not meant for eating. The principle to be followed is ahimsa, non-killing even for food. Saint Paul has endorsed this when he preached that 'It is good neither to eat flesh, nor to drink wine."

(4) **Madhyam:** "Madhyam masthaka sambutham" is a thanthric version which means that madhyam is produced from midbrow. This is the nectar of Divine grace resulting from the concentration of the mind at the heart centre. The yogi gets into a state of Brahmanandam intoxicated with the nectar of Divine grace. Sufis call this as a state of musth. This is symbolically represented by the nectar pot held in the curve of the trunks of Ganesha images with trunks turning right or hanging down straight.

(5) **Maithunam:** This is a metaphor indicating the merger of the mind with soul which is the end and aim of the sadhaka. This merger is analogous to the merger of sakti with Shiva. Maithunam, in the Panchamakaram concept is not sexual union.

In utter disregard of these sublime concepts conveyed by the five constituents of the Panchamakara thathwa of the saktha cult, people took them in the ordinary meanings and began to indulge in reprehensible practices. Mudra is interpreted as gram, Mathsyam is interpreted as fish, Mamsam is interpreted as flesh, Madhyam is interpreted as liquor and Maithunam is interpreted as sexual union. This twisted and perverted interpretation has resulted in a gluttonous orgy of eating cooked gram with fish and meat, helped by sumptuous quantity of liquor at the rituals and the ceremony would up by sexual indulgence by the devotees rituals and the ceremony would up by sexual indulgence by the devotees among themselves. This is religion taking a wrong turn as was the case with the carpocratian sect of the early christian church who equated christian morality with sexual religious rite.

Panchamakaram is to be understood as a system of progressive spiritual training beginning from the discipline of the Mudra and passing through the stages of control over mind and body and then on to the stage of supreme bliss and finally ending in a state of non-dualism or Adwaita. Those who are addicted to external mada, maithuna and mamsam go to hell. This is said by Mathangisanatha one of the teachers of the Mathsendranath School of thought in the following lines:

> "Bahrmada ratho yasthu maithune mamsa bakshane
> thesarvam narakam yanthi satyam vache mama."

The ancient seers of India had an uncanny ability of spotlighting the core of many psychic centres inside the brain. The modern medical sciences has testified to this their amazing ability which has been responsible for the formulation of the science of yoga. In the writings about yoga there are references about a lotus with thousand petals and a lotus heart. The lotus referred to, is the brain and the lotus heart is the neural heart within it, which is said to be the seat of Divinity in man. The lotus motif of the Hindu and Buddhist icons and the expression Manipadma (lotus jewel) in the Baddha manthra "Om Manipadme Hum" have reference to this metaphor of the lotus heart in man, the jewel being the life principle within.

Western philosophers and scientists have recognised that there are vital centres inside the brain like Pineal and Pituitary glands and other glandular bodies like thalamus and hypothalamus which perform important functions in human activity. The great philosopher Descartes held the view that pineal gland is the seat of the soul and before him St. Paul obviously referring to this brain centre said, it is the temple of God where the spirit of God dwelleth. The Bible dictionary gives the meaning of pineal as the face of god. The function of the pineal gland which is situated almost at the centre of the brain is not yet fully ascertained. It is believed that it has something to do with procreation and that may be the reason why it is called pineal which lends itself to an interpretation as the penis which is EL. The penis here is the neural penis. 'EL' means God or creative power. This agrees with the notion of the Hindus that Shiva linga is situated in the lotus heart inside the brain on a level with the middle of the brow.

The biologist Oscar Bagnell thinks that the pineal gland is associated with ultra violet reception in thought transmission or telepathy and Arthur Lammers and Edgar Cace, two psychic investigators, agreed with Descartes that the pineal gland is the seat of subconscious or soul mind while the pituitary gland is the seat of conscious mind.

The pituitary gland is situated below the pineal gland in close proximity with thalamus and hypothalamus bodies and the region of the medulla oblongata on a level with the mid point of the eye brows. It contains two lobes, the anterior and posterior. The anterior lobe is formed from the ectoderm of the roof of the mouth and the posterior lobe is the downward growth from the brain. Though no larger than a pea, this gland produces a whole battery of powerful hormones which act on the tissues of the body and other glands. If the anterior portion is sub-normal, it retards growth. If it is abnormal, it increases growth resulting in gigantism. The posterior portion of the gland produces pitutrine which tones up and controls kidneys, intestines and capillaries. For the above reasons, pituitary gland is considered as the master gland of the body. (See Sketch No.3).

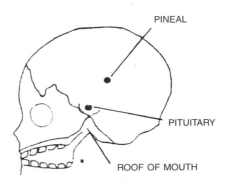

Sketch No. 3

Regarding thalamus and hypothalamus, Demitry Chebotaryov Director of the Institute of Gerentology, Soviet Union, says that this tiny section of the brain covered by these bodies have revealed many surprising details regarding the advent of old age and that this tiny area is the border of the two worlds viz., the outer world in which we live and the inner world of our body in which we think. Through the nervous system, the hypothalamus is said to obtain information from outside and passes it on to the endocrine system either along nerve channels or with the aid of hormones.

It may be noted that the pineal, the pituitary and thalamus bodies are situated in the core of the brain situated above the medulla oblongata which is identified is the Muladharam of which Ganesha is said to be the presiding deity, and some

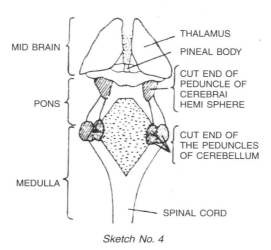

MID BRAIN

PONS

MEDULLA

THALAMUS

PINEAL BODY

CUT END OF
PEDUNCLE OF
CEREBRAI
HEMI SPHERE

CUT END OF
THE PEDUNCLES
OF CEREBELLUM

SPINAL CORD

Sketch No. 4

knowledge about these powerful brain centres vis-a-vis the various mystical terms bearing on certain psychic centres in the brain may be useful in this critical study of Ganesha. (See Sketch No.4).

The core of the brain is considered as Brama Randram meaning the hole of Brahma, the Sanctum sanctorum of the temple of God. This temple is said to have nine doors. A mistake is made here also in the matter of the identification of these nine gates. Two eyes, two nostrils, two ears, a mouth, an anus and an urethra are said to be the nine gates. These cannot be accepted as the nine gates for the reason that a female has an extra gate leading to her womb. There cannot be any distinction, between man and woman so far as yoga and metaphysics are concerned. Moreover the urethra, anus and the passage to the womb are ejective organs and these cannot be considered as gates to the city of God in man. Two eyes, two ears, two nostrils and a mouth constitute seven gates. For the location of the remaining two gates we have to look to the head and no where else. The writer has been told by his guru that these two gates are two ducts perceptible to clairvoyant vision, running up to Brahma Randhram from both sides of the sthalu (uvula) obviously in the direction of the ectoderm of the roof of mouth serving the pituitary, Thalamus and Pineal bodies. By constant practice of pranayam, prana in the upward movement as the breath of life, stimulates the glandular regions above ectoderm of the roof of the mouth, bringing about an exalted feeling of delight to the sadhaka. The two hidden ducts get opened and the sadhaka is now on the high road to samadhi. (See Sketch No.3).

In certain images of Ganesha there is a third eye situated in the middle of the brow. This eye is the symbol of enlightenment and realisation of the brow-man, the Brahman. Significantly enough this eye of Ganesha occupies a space in level with the space covered by the pineal, pituitary and thalamus bodies which constitutes the lotus heart the seat of Brahman or god. The wearing of a mark mid brow by Hindus originated as a pious reminder of this sanctum sanctorum of Brahman in the lotus heart. In course of time people lost sight of the real object and the mark degenerated into a symbol of narrow sectarianism in the case of men and exhibitionism and silly make up in the case of women who started matching the colour of this mark with the dress they wear.

There is yet another mystic syllable 'OM' held sacred by all Hindus and Buddhists with which Ganesha is very much connected. This is dealt with separately in the next chapter.

Five headed Ganesha made of country teak Vangai wood from Kalakorchi village in Tamilnadu

Three headed Ganesha made of country teak Vangai wood from Kalakorchi village – Tamilnadu

GANESHA AND 'OM'

 In the Ganapathyopanishad Ganesha is described as the form of Turiya indicated by 'omkara' (form of 'OM') abiding in the Muladharam. This is an abstract metaphysical statement. We have studied something about Muladharam and now we have to study something about 'OMKARA' to appreciate the description of Ganesha given in the Ganapathyopanishad.

Mandukyopanishad speaks about 'OM' as follows:

"OM Ithiekaksharamitham sarvam, thasyopa vyakyanam, butham bavath bavishyabhithi sarva omkara mevachanyath thrikalathitham thadpyomkara eva."

The gist of the above verse is as follows:

All this world is of the form 'OM'. In further explanation, the past, present and future are all 'OM'. And whatever transcends the three divisions of time, is also 'OM'. This upanishad identifies 'OM' as brahman or atman which manifests itself in four states, viz. (1) the waking state (2) the dreaming state (3) the state of the deep sleep and (4) the state of super consciousness. 'OM' is universally accepted by Hindus and even by Buddhists as the sound symbol of the supreme power which can be analysed into three sound elements viz. 'A' 'U' and 'M'.

The sound element 'A' is indicative of the waking state, 'U' of the dream state and 'M' of the deep sleep state.

The waking state represented by the sound element 'A' is the outwardly cognitive world, which is ephemeral and which is sustained by the ego. The dream state represented by the sound element 'U' is also a world but inwardly cognitive which is also ephemeral and sustained by the ego. The events in the world of dream state appear as much realistic as they appear in the world of the waking state. The feeling that the dream events appear to be lasting only for a short time, while events in the waking state appear to last longer is brought about by confounding the standard of time in the waking state which the standard of time in the dream state which differ from each other.

Descartes says in his Meditations "The visions of a dream and the experience of my waking state are so much alike that I do not really know I am not dreaming at this moment." On a minute analysis of these two states it will become clear that they are not inconsistent or contradictory states of existence. The waking state which is not permanent disappears into the dream state and dream state which is also not permanent disappears into the dream state and dream state which is also not permanent disappears in dreamless sleep which is represented by the sound element 'M'. One in deep sleep feels no desires and sees no dreams.

It is a spiritual condition where the experiences of the waking and dream states are dissolved but not destroyed. We like a good sleep without dreams because it is a state of bliss. The state of deep sleep is called Prajna which is equated with Isvara, the Lord of All. Just as from Iswara springs up the whole universe, so also from the consciousness in deep sleep springs the whole phenomenon of dream and waking states. Shakespeare touched the fringes of the reality when he wrote "we are such stuff as dreams are made of'. There is a fourth state transcending the sound symbol 'OM'. This state is the soundless aspect of 'OM' called by the name Turiyam. Turiyam is also understood to be the state of sat-cit-ananda or existence - knowledge — bliss. The above mentioned notes though meagre, regarding 'OM' and its three sound elements and Turiyam its soundless aspect, may be useful to understand the concept of Ganesha envisaged in the Ganapathyopanishad.

In the Vainayakapurana known also as Bharagavapurana, Ganesha is described as the creator of everything including Brahma, Vishnu and Shiva. This is a paradox for the reason that Ganesha is considered to be the son of Shiva. Perhaps in the realm of absolute values where abstract and spiritual concepts are involved causes and effects efface themselves or this may be due to the fact that his sectarian devotees boosted him up to occupy a position above the Trinity taking advantage of the story that he had come into existence without the intervention of Shiva, his mother's consort.

Sketch No. 5

The sound symbol 'OM' of the Absolute is said to be the form of Ganesha. 'OM' is the Pranava Nadam, the Anahatha vibration and the name Ganesha, a modified form of Kanesha meaning the lord of sound, is most appropriate for this Deity. This concept is beyond the comprehension of ordinary undeveloped minds. So it has been given a symbol in the manner of an alphabet preserved both in Dravidian Tamil and Aryan Sanskrit in the shapes as found on the next page.

These two symbol letters one in Tamil and the other in Sanskrit resemble the profile of the head of an elephant which is adopted by Ganesha for this head. This can be made out in Ganesha figures with trunks turning towards right and for this reason such figures go by the name of 'Omkara Ganapathy'. (See Sketch).

A similar process of formation of a symbol letter appears to have been followed in the Hebrew language. No language is possible without the sound element 'A' or 'Akara'. So it forms the first letter in all languages. In Hebrew the first letter is 'Aleph'. Aleph is the semitic name for a bull which was considered as a sacred animal in all ancient countries. Obviously, the first letter in Hebrew 'Aleph' was formed in honour of this sacred animal. The origin of the present English letter 'A' which is in the shape of the inverted head of a bull can be traced to this Hebrew origin. Perhaps, John Bull the nick-name of the English men may be an inheritance from the Hebrew through this alphabetical source.

A sage by name Akathisan (God within) popularly known as 'Agasthyar' is said to have brought the prevedic cult of yoga down to the south when the Aryan invaders drove away the original desis (natives of the soil). Sage Agasthyar maintained and kept up the high traditions of the Tamil language and culture and so he is considered as the patron sage of Tamil Language. The Tamil form of writing 'OM' which was also adopted by the Sanskrit was invented by this sage.

It may be noted that both in the Tamil form and in the Sanskrit form of writing 'OM' a similarity in features like the forehead, single tusk and trunk with bent towards right as seen in Ganesha images is prominent. This similarity appears to have been brought about to identify them with the mystic syllable 'OM'. The writing 'OM' itself is a compendious mark of a profound thought and the image of Ganesha is an elaborate symbol of this profound thought attracting universal attention in its silent eloquence.

The great siddha saints have described the flow of Ida Nadi (flow out of breath) as extending up to twelve digits from the lower end of the nose and the way of attaining samadhi is to control and regulate this flow. Verily the trunk of Ganesha represents this invisible flow of breath which is responsible for the phenomenal world.

This Vaishnava Hindus of South India who worship God as Vishnu and his several incarnations gave prominence to Twelve Alwars who had become Godmen and notwithstanding Ganesha's Saiva affiliation, he was also personified and called Thumbikai Alwar (The Alwarwith a trunk) and worshipped and given prominence as Deity to be propitiated for the removal of all obstacles in life.

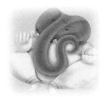

Shri Girijatmaj – Lenyadri

GANESHA AND THE HINDU PANTHEON

Although the Aryan invaders derided Shiva, the Dravidian God and the parent of Ganesha as Sishna Deva (Phallus God) and made the Holy Elephant as the mount of their chief God Indra, in subsequent years, the Aryan people from the land of Iran began to recognise the greatness of the prevedic culture. With this recognition Shiva became an important God, replacing Indra and the title of Ganapathy indicating the lord of hosts used by Indra was conferred on Shiva also. Not long after, Ganesha who was already a prevedic Deity and who had a good deal of esoteric metamorphosis forced himself into the Hindu pantheon appropriating the title of Ganapathy exclusively for himself. By this time, Indra the Chief of the Gods of the Aryans, degenerated himself into a philanderer. In one of his foolish sprees he got into a mess with sage Gauthama's Wife whom he seduced under impersonation. As a reprisal Gauthama effectively cursed him with a dire affliction of having female organs all over his body. Indra went into hiding and being told that only Ganesha will be able to cure him of this unseemly malady, he prayed to Ganesha for a cure. Ganesha appeared before him in answer to his prayer and initiated him into the practice of yoga. Indra practiced yoga implicitly following Ganesha's advice and thanks to the power of yoga, he became his former self again. Shiva had already been recognised as the lord of yoga and this legend besides recognising Ganesha as another lord of yoga is also designed to show the superiority of yoga practice over the ritualism of yaga, of which Indra is considered as a patron. In this legend, importance is given to Ganesha and not to Shiva by Indra and this made Ganesha as the universal God. His devotees began to call him by a thousand names, each name denoting a divine attribute that he is said to represent. His image also became an object of worship with elaborate rites.

This is idolatry not in keeping with the yoga ideology which Ganesha is supposed to represent. But the protagonists of idolatry say that the idol worship is not bad for the reason that the dedicated idol is held to be the abode of super human personality or the symbol of a great ideal or thought which makes it different from the statue or a piece of art, or a lump of clay or stone. This argument though plausible may not be sound as it is made on the assumption that such idols require worship and this worship is the sum total of all virtues. It is such arguments that made many Buddhists to take to the worship of Buddha's idol instead of following he moral principles laid down by him. Many worshippers of Ganesha also have fallen into a similar morass losing sight of the spiritual concepts that he stands for.

Ganesha is anthropocentric i.e. centering the universe in himself, and his idographic image is the image of a cosmic man conceived by man in a grotesque form. This cosmic man has power to project the world and withdraw the same at his will. He is the presiding Deity of the Muladhara depicted as sitting on a mouse which is considered a mystic animal in many countries. In certain depictions the mouse is seen merrily eating the sweet cakes given to its master by his devotees. The selection of this frail and tiny rodent as a mount for Ganesha perforce, is of great significance.

The thoracic cavity of the human body contains the fleshy heart and lungs which are controlled by the Medulla oblongata. The lungs occupy a greater part of its space. The lungs besides helping the respiratory process, maintain the flow of the breath of life steady and constant to play the rhythmic tune of life as 'Ham' and 'Sam' just as the bag of bagpipe maintains the supply of air to the reed producing the music steady and constant so that the rhythm and melody of the music does not get intermittent or get snapped in the course of the piper's performance. Thoracic cavity is called moochakam in Dravidian Tamil. Mooch means the breath of life. Akam means a room or closet. Moochakam therefore refers to the room or closet where the breath of life is tuned and conditioned for phenomenal manifestation. If the breath of life snaps or gets severed from its internal mooring, the life will become extinct. If it is controlled or withdrawn from its usual activity, it remains in a state like that of suspended animation as in the case of a foetus floating in a pool of amniotic fluid in its mother's womb, reminiscent of God Narayana floating on the face of waters before creation.

The foetus in the mother's womb has life, its heart beats, but it does not breath, though endowed with a pair of lungs. The foetus has no world. The world appears as its own creation when it comes out of the womb and its prana begins to function through its four agencies, viz. mind, chitham, buddhi and ahamkaram. These four agencies are symbolised in mythology as the four faces of Brahma the creator.

Moochakam (The Thoracic Cavity) enclosing the lungs and fleshy heart is represented by the mouse as its symbol.

The medulla oblongata which is the controlling authority of breathing and heart beat situated above the thoracic cavity is represented by Ganesha as its symbol. We have noted that medulla oblongata can be identified with Muladhara of which Ganesha is said to be the presiding deity. This is the significance of Ganesha and his mount, the mouse, which is called in Sanskrit 'Mushikam', a corruption of Moochakam. (See Sketch No.6).

Although Ganesha who was a prevedic Deity was admitted into the post vedic Hindu pantheon, it would seem that there was no organised cult of Ganesha worship before the Gupta period. The cult as well as the Ganesha idols with its several facets of psychic concepts were evolved over a long period of time

Sketch No. 6

beginning from the prehistoric days. Ganesha appears to have acquired his platonic consorts only after the development of Tantra cult both by the Hindus and by the Buddhists. Buddhists associated Ganesha with Bodisathva in the text of their Vinayaka Sutha. But an intercult rivalry among the vajrayana thantric Buddhists cropped up, as a result of which Ganesha idols were thrown off their pedestals. In some works of art Ganesha is trampled down by Manjushree the Bodisatwa of great wisdom. This is sectarian intolerance. Such intolerance was also shown to Ganesha by the followers of St. Xavier of Goa. There are some pictures drawn by the followers of St. Xavier where Ganesha idols are shown pulled off their pedestals and thrown in the gutter in the presence of the saint himself. St. Xavier was a siddha. He would not have countenanced any such offensive evangelism. The pictures may be spurious publications by his overzealous followers long after his samadhi. But whatever it may be Ganesha withstood all these insults and onslaughts and is still seen in all glory.

The Hindus never let him down. In all religious forms of worship, he is the first Deity to be supplicated to remove all obstacles. Adi Shankara though not an idolater himself included him among the five Deities, viz. Surya, Shiva, Vishnu, Ganesh and Ambal to be worshipped by people who are not able to comprehend the higher concepts of yoga philosophy or conceive God in abstract terms.

By about the 10th century A.D. Ganesha became a very powerful Deity. The Ganapathya sect came into prominence with the cult of pancha Ganapathy viz. (1) The Uchista Ganapathy (2) Maha Ganapathy (3) Urdhava Ganapathy (4) Pingala Ganapathy (5) Lakshmi Ganapathy. The Ganapathy a sect considered Ganesha as the first cause, through whose maya, Shiva and other Gods were created. He was worshipped both by devotional and contemplative practices. In course of time the Ganapathya sect got degenerated and began to indulge in abominable practices and licentious ceremonies. Ganesha was given a third consort to improve his status in addition to his other two platonic consorts Buddhi and Siddhi. This third consort by name Vallabha does not appear to be satisfied by platonic love. In the contemporary idols Ganesha's trunk is seen probing her private part and the gesture is reciprocated by her, by holding

Ganesha's private part in her hand. These obscene figures also were put up for worship. The Ganapathya sect did not survive long, after this moral degradation. The sect got disintegrated. But Ganesha survived this Ordeal of odium cast on his idols and is seen still occupying the hearts of his ardent devotees.

From India worship has been carried not only to neighbouring countries but also to distant countries like China, Japan and Mongolia. Recently a figure of Ganesha was unearthed in a village near Sofia in Bulgaria along with the figures of Buddha and Mahavira.

In China Ganesha is accepted in his spiritual aspect as Vajradhathu and in his material aspect of garbhadathu. In Japan he is called Vajara Vinayaka in double form, one male and other female known as Kangi and Ten. Japanese consider these figures as of great esoteric significance and worship them in secret. The worship of Ganesha in China and Japan appears to be due to the influence of Thantric Buddhism.

The Mongolians also adored Ganesha through the influence of the Chinese. There is a story in extant that Emperor Kublai Khan's father was childless and he was advised to pray to Ganesha to bless him with a son. The prayer bore fruit and the childless father was blessed with a son who became the illustrious Kublai Khan. The influence of Ganesha did not last long in Mongolia. Ganesha figures also have been unearthed in Mexico. There must have been some communication between India and Mexico as otherwise it will be difficult to explain how the idols of Ganesha reached Mexico. In 1868 Father Zumloohm discovered in Easter Inland in Pacific Ocean a number of wooden Tablets called Kohan Mongo (new boards) which were covered with script signs. The Hungarian Scholar Hevesy recognised a startling resemblance between their Easter Island script and Indus Valley script and he thinks that the script followed migrations from South East Asia. Such being the case there is nothing improbable if we say that Ganesha also followed migrations from South East Asia and reached Mexico. It is for the research scholars to find out how Ganesha reached Mexico and how he fared there.

Sculptor at work

Rosewood Base, yellow Teakwood from Kerala – work done in Mysore village

GANESHA AND HIS IDOL

The prominent features in the idol of Ganesha is his Elephant head. Elephant is the biggest mammal of the land referred to in Hindu religious and other literature as gajam. Gajanana (elephant faced) is one of the names of Ganesha. Gaja is not a vedic word. In order to understand the esoteric significance of this word we have to study this word side by side with the vedic word Ajam or Aja.

Ordinarily Aja means a goat but esoterically it means that which is not born indicating the infinite Brahman a negative name for a positive principle which is the repository of Nada Bindu and Kala. We have noted that Kala is the creative force and Bindu is an impulse from the creative force and Nada is the sound vibrations from which the phenomenal world appears. Nada is also called by the name of gao. The word Govinda is familiar to all Hindus as the name of God the creator of world. Govinda is made up of two concepts viz. 'Gao' meaning Nada and 'Bindu' meaning the impulse from Kala, the creative force. According to the Amara Kosa earth is also called by the name 'Gao' signifying that it is materialisation of sound (Nada) vibrations.

Ordinarily gajam means an elephant. But esoterically it means earth which is born of gao. 'Gao' as already mentioned means Nada. 'Jam' means that which is born. 'Ajam' meaning that which is not born is infinite. It has no form. It is pure spirit. Whereas gajam symbolising the materialised world is finite. It has form and gajam the elephant is fitted in as an apt and meaningful symbol for this materialised world. This symbolic meaning is a latter day development and the elephant has thus secured a place of importance in the puranas of the Hindus.

In puranic mythology abstract concepts are personified and woven into stories for the edification of common people and the symbols of elephants are very much significantly used for this purpose as the Carrytides of the earth by assigning them this grand role. Eight elephants known as Dikgajams are said to be carrying the earth on their backs, four of them occupying the four cardinal points and four others occupying the four intermediary points. The collapse of these carrytides mean the collapse of the world.

Yoga aims at the complete withdrawal of the self or ego from the world of its creation. In symbolic language it is the annihilation of the elephant or varana nasam. Varanam is another name for elephant and its nasam means, its destruction. Varananasam was corrupted as Varanasi and the name was adopted for a great centre of learning disseminating esoteric knowledge on the banks of Ganges which at present goes by the name of Benaras. This centre is also called as Kasi which means enlightenment. Buddha preached his first sermon near about this centre. Adi Sankara established a mutt there to preach his Adwaitha philosophy. In course of time Varanasi which taught people how to annihilate the elephant lost its sanctity and became infested with unscrupulous pandas and credulous pilgrims. The pilgrims do not crave for any learning. They go there to have a dip in the Ganges in the hope that they would go to heaven.

On the banks of Ganges there is another Kasi on the Himalayan heights known as Uttar Kasi visited by many pilgrims. This mountain height bears the name of Varanavatham which also means the destruction of the elephant. The names Varanasi and Varana Vatham are not there by accident. These names are deliberately given as symbol names to denote the sublime ideal underlying the destruction of the elephant.

The allegory symbolised by the killing of the elephant is also narrated in the story of Krishna destroying Kuvalayapitam (support of the world) the terrible tusker owned by the egoist Kamsa. Krishna in another story plays the role of saving Gajendra from the clutches of a crocodile. Gajendra in this story is the reincarnation of the egoistic Pandya King Indra Dyumna who was cursed by sage Agastya to be born as a elephant. It may be noted that the destruction of Kuvalayapitam and its master is a purposeful annihilation like the complete destruction of Gomorrah and Sodom by God. There was no other go. The people there were so wicked. But Gajendra was saved as a result of its fervent prayer to the lord and the consequent downpour of his grace which is a fundamental doctrine of the Hindu Dharma. The taming of Madagiri, the mad elephant, by Buddha is another allegory of a different nature to show how enlightenment of mind could be used to bring peace to the mad humanity. Shiva the Lord of Yoga is wearing an elephant skin. Shiva is also called Gajari meaning the Killer of the Elephant, esoterically meaning the annihilation of the Ego. The ceremony of carrying the image of God on the back of the elephant in Hindu Temples is to remind people that God is the Lord of the Earth, the earth being represented by the Elephant.

This dissertation on the significance of the elephant and its use or destruction is pertinent for a critical study of Ganesha for the reason that Ganesha idols are seen dominated by the head of the elephant. This makes the idols of Ganesha, prima facie represent the material world of which the elephant is the symbol. But since only the head of the elephant is preferred and incorporated in Ganesha idols to the exclusion of the rest of its body, this preference is significant, and the idols have to be studied in the light of this preference. Ganesha being a male deity the head chosen for him is the head of a tusker. The most peculiar organ seen in this head is its prehensile nose called trunk. In all beings the breath of life is the connecting link between the individual being and its relative world. The elephant is no exception. The nose of the elephant is peculiarly a movable organ. This organ generally is seen hanging down. But it can be moved either to the left or right, or lifted up, without any impediment to the breath of life or the breathing process.

In some idols of Ganesha the trunks hangs down straight. In some, they either turn towards the left side or right side. These variations are not made in any haphazard manner. There is some meaning with regard to these variations. Although it is not correct to identify Ida Nadi with the flow of breath in the left nostril and Pingala Nadi with the flow of breath in the right nostril a convention appears to have been established in iconography, to consider the left side of the idol of Ganesha as expressive of the flow of Ida and the right side as

Sketch No. 7

expressive of the flow of Pingala. In any idol of Ganesha if the trunk is hanging straight down it is indicative of the unmanifested static reservoir of energy called Sushumna. If the trunk is seen turning towards the left it is indicative of the flow of Ida. If it is seen turning towards right it is indicative of the flow of Pingala. The trunk turning towards the left side is invariably seen reaching a bowl of

modhaka (Laddus) which is indicative of the material involvement of the mind in motion through the sense organs. The trunks hanging down straight or turning towards right are seen in some idols carrying a pot of nectar in the curve of their trunks. This is indicative of the soul's attainment of immortality. (See Sketch No. 7 & 8).

Ganesha figures with trunks turning towards the right are called Valampiri Vinayakar. In South India many important temples have Valampiri Vinayakar. In Kalady close to the place where Adi Shankara's mother was supposed to have been cremated, there is an idol of Valampiri Vinayakar. Trunks turning towards right is the symbol of the mind's spiritual progress through the savya or Devayana path of light, highly commended by Adi Shankara himself.

Sketch No. 8

There are images of Ganesha with his left leg resting on a mouse and his right leg lifted up. Mouse represents the Moochakam, the Power house of the breath of life. The left leg of Ganesha resting on the mouse should be interpreted as exercising control over the flow of breath of life as Ida Nadi which is responsible for the appearance of the phenomenal world. The lifted right leg should be interpreted as an effort of the mind to soar up through Pingala Nadi towards Sushumna, the brood house of the serpent energy. In some images Ganesha's left leg is found resting on a mouse and his right leg on a lion. Lion is the mount of Ganesha's immaculate mother and a symbol of Pingala Nadi. The left leg on the mouse and the right leg on the lion is the neutralisation of the Ida and Pingala, process in the pranayam practice. In some images Ganesha's mount is seen carrying a jewel in its mouth. This jewel is chintamani meaning mental illumination or enlightenment, to be attained by the practice of pranayam and other meditational methods.

Originally Ganesha had only two hands just like ordinary mortals. Later on two more hands were added to distinguish him from ordinary mortals. In course of time more hands were added, each hand carrying an object different from the other. These several objects carried in the hands are also symbol marks of certain metaphysical concepts as picked up by his devotees from his all inclusive nature. The most popular form of Ganesha is the four handed one. Two hands are lower and two are upper. The two lower hands of which one is with palm pointing downwards is an offer to his devotees of refuge and the other with palm pointing upwards is a promise of protection and showering of grace on the refugee. Obviously, these two hands presenting Abhaya and Varada mudras depict the influence of the cult like Vaishnava cult upholding the doctrine of absolute surrender and doctrine of grace. The two upper hands of which one holds a elephant hook (Ankusa) is a symbol of selective faculty in choosing what is enabling curbing the evil tendencies of the mind, and the other which holds a rope (pasa) is a symbol of bond or worldly attachment. It is emblematic of the enlightenment after the bonds of attachment are broken.

There are dancing idols of Ganesha. Although ordinary eyes cannot meet in Ganesha's dance anything more than what a circus elephant can perform, a discerning eye can discover the colossal rhythmic flow of life as Ida and Pingala. The world appears and disappears in between the pacings of his left and right feet. Ganesha's dance in this respect is similar to the dance of Shiva, but with an difference. Shiva's dance appears much more graceful. For this the artist who wrought his icon is alone responsible. The dance of Ganesha is the expression of the underlying unity and rhythm in all material manifestations however gross or grotesque they may appear to the ordinary eye. (See sketch No. 9 & 10).

Ganesha idols are seen only with one tusk. The other tusk is seen broken. The broken tusk speaks a lot. In Hindu iconography there is a figure depicting the incarnation of Mahavishnu as Varaha (wild boar). The world represented as a globe is seen resting on its two tusks. Although the name Varaha means a wild boar, this name has an esoteric meaning as revealed by the two concepts with which the name is formed. One is 'Vara' meaning wedded to, and the other concept is 'Aham' which means self or ego. Varaham therefore means one wedded to one's ego. In astrological parlance Ahamkara or Angaraka (Mars) is the Karaka (cause) for the appearance of the world. The tusks of the boar indicates the ego and its relative world, YOU and I, a dualistic existence. The dualism disappears when the mind wedded to the ego sheds the ego. This destruction of YOU and I disappears. The broken tusk of Ganesha is the symbol of the shedding of the ego and the remaining single tusk indicates the nondualistic aspect of the mind when it gets merged with the Atman within, effacing the phenomenal world. Ganesha in this respect is Ekadanta (He of single tusk). The legend of Ganesha breaking one of his tusk to use it as a weapon to annihilate the elephant faced Gajamukhasura has a bearing on this aspect of Ganesha. It may be noted that Gajamukhasura is a demon with an elephant face whereas Ganesha who is also called Gajanana meaning elephant faced is a Deity. The annihilation of the demon in the annihilation of the elephant the mind slaying the ego which is sustained by its lower side.

In some idols Ganesha is depicted as having two heads. They are called dwimukha Ganesha. These

Sketch No. 9

Sketch No. 10

two heads are symbols of his microcosmic and macrocosmic aspects known in Hindu philosophy and religion as pindandam and Brahmandam.

It may be noted that in esoteric Hinduism the human body with its mind is considered as a miniature or replica of the world outside. The forces which govern the microcosm and operate on it, also govern and operate the macrocosm. Such being the case by certain mental and physical processes, the yogi can win for himself not only supernatural powers over his own body and mind, but also a micraculous control over the outer world. The three headed Ganesha represents the three strands of qualities, Sathwa, Rajas and Tamas inherent in nature. The four headed Ganesha represents Mind, Chitham, Buddhi and Ahamkaram the four psychic aspects of Brahma the creator of the world who also is depicted in iconography with four faces.

The five headed Ganesha figures may signify a multiplicity of concepts all expressed in terms of five factors. It may represent the five maha Bhuthas with their relative sensory organs or it may mean the five sheaths of kosha like (1) The Annamaya Kosha (2) The Pranamaya Kosha (3) The Manomaya Kosha (4) The Vignanamaya Kosha (5) The Anandamaya Kosha. Generally, the Annamaya Kosha is interpreted as the physical built by food. This may not be the esoteric interpretation. The correct interpretation lies in the direction of the underlying principle in the human system for converting the food as energy for sustaining the Prana in its movement as outgoing and incoming breath of life to manifest the phenomenal world.

Annam is the Hamsam the cosmic swan meaning the breath of life. From breath of life you go back to Prana, from Prana to mind, from mind to the supreme truth vignana and thence to Anand (sat-chit-Anand). The fifth head sat-chit-Anand is found in the middle, with the other four heads distributed, one at each cardinal point from the head in the middle. In the Sat-chit-Ananda conception, Sat is the infinite real, Chith is the consciousness and Ananda is the supreme bliss.

The five heads may also mean the five Brahmas as described in the Pancha Brahmopanishad, Shiva was credited with these heads, viz. (1) Sadyojatha (2) Aghora (3) Vama Deva (4) Tat Purusha (5) Isana. When Ganesha became more powerful than Shiva his devotees may have invested him with these five heads. This is only speculation.

The writer is of the view that out of the above three sets of five heads, the interpretation regarding the set pertaining to the Koshas (sheaths) may be appropriate for Ganesha figures with five heads.

The additions in features and other changes in the idols of Ganesha appear to have been necessitated by the development of Agama culture in the Hindu religion, which appealed to the imagination of the ordinary class of Hindu population. Agama sastras laid down prescriptions for the worship of idols in temples. It encouraged the instilling of a belief in the common mind that God has taken incarnation in the idol. Obviously Ganesha idols also got invested with such an incarnation idea of God acceptable to the followers of different sects in the Hindu society.

The Hindu temples have now become Ganesha's strong holds from where it is difficult to dislodge him.

GANESHA AND HIS LAMBODARAM

*T*he advent of Agama Sastras made the practice of religion easy for the Hindus. The elaborate ritualism of the vedas and the exacting discipline of the yoga path were obviated by a simple process of idol worship either at home or outside, in temples. Vedanta conceived God as one without form but people started giving him forms according to their mental developments and tendencies. Some gave him animal forms, some gave him human forms and some gave him mixed forms and some represented him in geometrical patterns. Ganesha comes under the mixed form.

These diverse ways of thinking and shaping of Gods arose more out of a desire to satisfy a pristine and innocent urge in men than out of any wanton profanity. But it is unfortunate that the credulity of these innocents is being exploited by some others who are unscrupulous for purposes which may very well be described as profane. God does not want idols or worship. God is an immaculate law and knowledge of this law and obeying the law would be more than sufficient to please Him. This is high thinking. But people at lower levels caught in the grip of their own psychic aberrations require some refuge and the several Gods, their idols and symbols all constitute such a refuge set up for their psychic needs even as they put up shelters variously improvised as refuge for their physical needs from the vagaries of weather.

Ganesha has in this sense become a stupendous edifice for such people to take shelter. This edifice was begun in prehistorical days and completed after a lapse of several centuries. For people in the elementary stage of thinking, Ganesha is a refuge. But for people with higher knowledge he is a picture writing of philosophy and mysticism as could be made out by the following prayer addressed to him.

> "Eka Dantam maha kayam
> thapta kanchana sannibham
> Lambodaram Visalaksham
> Vandeham Gananayakam."

Ganesha is described in this prayer as lord of gana and as having a single tusk, a huge body of the colour of molten gold with a big belly and broad eyes. This prayer is composed evidently by a master mind, with much esoteric significance behind it. The body of Ganesha is described as huge and as such there is no need to mention again anything about the belly for belly is part of the body unless it be that the word "Lambodaram" is purposely meant to convey a particular meaning. As ordinarily understood Lambodharam means a belly which is long or big.

In the esoteric astronomy, there are two paths of the solar disc distinguished as Uthara (North) and Dhakshina (South). The word Uthara contains two concepts. One is the concept conveyed by the sound element 'U' and the other is the concept conveyed by the word 'Tara'. We have noted that the sound element 'U' of 'OM' is symbolic of the dream state of the mind, which is inwardly cognitive. The word 'Tara' means path. Uthara therefore means the path indicated by the sound element of 'U'. This is the inward movement of the Prana, the functioning of Pingala Nadi which is the savya path of light which is followed by yogis. The end of this path is indicated by the sound element 'M' in 'OM' which is the state of Prajna. The Dakshina path is the Apasavya path sought after by worldly men. The great pithamaha Bhishma of the Maha Bharatha story, though mortally wounded waited by the power of his own yoga sakthi, to give up his ghost till the advent of utharayana (Northern course of the Sun) as that period was considered to be an auspicious period for people to die.

The death bed episode of Bhishma should be understood in an esoteric sense. The ego withdraws itself from the world of its own creation and takes to the Devayana path indicated by the sound element of 'U' of (OM) to the infinite point of bliss indicated by the sound element of 'm' of (OM). If the meaning is taken in the ordinary sense then any sinner will be getting salvation if he happens to die in the course of the Northern movement of the Sun.

Udharam is ordinarily used to indicate the stomach. When we speak of Lambodharam it is understood to be the description of the pot belly of Ganesha as huge and long. This may be the impression that a superficial observer may get when he sees a Ganesha figure or think about it. But the description in the prayer of the udharam is not meant to be an assessment of the size of his physical belly. We have mentioned in chapter 9 that Ganesha is described in Ganapathyopanishad as the form of Turiya indicated by 'omkara'. The udharam meant in the prayer is a reference to the savyapath. The prefix 'lamba' to the word 'udharam' is only indicative of the length of time that one may take before he reaches his destination.

Visaalaksham or broad eyes do not indicate their size which are disproportionate to the size of the head of Ganesha. The description is only with reference to the breadth of his vision or its all seeing power. In some figures he is seen with a third eye in his fore head. Obviously this eye is the eye

Sketch No. 11

Ganesh Temple – Titwala, Bombay – before 2000

Ganesh Temple – Titwala, Bombay – in 2000

of spiritual insight or the eye of Brahma. Brahma should be understood as the "Brow-man" the divine principle located inside the brow region of every being. Regarding Eka dantam we have mentioned in Chapter 11 that it is the state of adwaita in symbol form.

The above mentioned prayer reveals that Ganesha is a yoga murthy. There is another prayer or hymn addressed to him which throws more light on his spiritual personality. The hymn in the nature of an invocation prayer is as follows:

> "Suklambaradharam Vishnum
> Sasivarnam Chathurbujam
> Prasannavadhanam Dhyayeth
> Sarva vignopa santhaye."

The superficial meaning of the hymn is as follows: He who is clothed in white, bright as a moon and having four hands with a pleasant face, may he protect us against all setbacks.

The expression 'Suklambaradharam Vishnum' is very significant. Suklambaram is not white cloth. The real meaning has to be ascertained. There is also no mention of Ganesha's tusk, trunk, belly and eyes. The superficial meaning as it is ordinarily understood by the common people would make him out a cheap bazar doll. But this hymn is being uttered by every pious Hindu in fervent devotion before he does anything. Even spiritual heads invoke this hymn believing in the potency of its invocation impregnated with the mystical concepts used therein.

Esoterically speaking this hymn invokes the help of Him (Ganesha) against all obstacles, referring him as the pure essence of luminous mind or all pervasive mind sky (Sukalambaradharam Vishnam) with four hands indicating his Divinity and the colour of moon indicating mental enlightenment, moon being the symbol of mind and a face beaming the beatitude. (See Figure Facing Page).

A little reflection of the inner meaning of the above hymn would reveal the pranava aspect of Ganesha. He is described not by his physical appearance but by the quality of his sublime nature which is Sat-Chith-Ananda and in this light Ganesha's face of beatitude (Prasannavadhanam) stands ineffable before a discerning eye. He in spite of his weird and funny looks presents himself as an ideal of spiritual pursuit and a compendium of esoteric knowledge. Many a sadhaka who has understood him has contemplated on him in his several aspects in the course of the practice of yoga and attained a state of bliss following the savya path of light indicated by his Lambodharam.

Shri Vighneshwar -- Ozar

The purport of the above verse is that the yogi sees God (Shiva) in his Atman and not in images. Images are meant only for ignorant people. Even here it may be wrong to think that the idol worshipper is treating God as an idol or stone. He obviously sees God in the idol or in the stone and sticks to it. God knows it all.

In the matter of worship of Ganesha people with lower development of mind take to worship of his idol. Development of mind is meant here as spiritual development. There are many intelligent people among the Hindus who worship idols. This they do by habit, custom and vested interests. They are very superficial in their approach to religion. People with spiritual development do not require the aid of an idol and if they respect an idol they see a meaning in it which is not discerned by ordinary minds. Such people do not worship Ganesha in his idol form. But they do contemplate on his ideology. They are different from iconoclasts who have done more disservice to religion and God than idolaters. Some collect Ganesha idols as curios. This is not bad for curiosity is the starting point of knowledge. But whatever it may be, there is no denial of the act that Ganesha attracts both overt ritualism and contemplative spiritualism. Ritualism can be with or without idols. It is seen in some form or other in all religions and appears to be a preliminary step for the votaries like the mother's milk for the baby. When the baby outgrows its mother's bosom it fends for itself. Ethics, aesthetics, mind control and right living are deliberate steps to attain maturity of mind in religious matters.

 Agnipuranam says:
"Uthama sahajavastha
Dwitiya Dhyana dharana
Thritiya pratima puja
Homa yatra vidambana"

The meaning of the above verse is as follows:

The best state of mind is to get into tune with the immortal infinite. The laboured contemplation of the infinite is next to this. Lower to this is fixing the mind to some material image; ritualism, offerings, sacrifices, pilgrimages and moving up and down of hands and feet are self deception mummery or past time.

Temple and other places where idols or symbols are kept for worship are likened to kindergarten schools with their toys, pictures and abacus to train little children. When they grow up they avoid these and stand on their own mental ability. Grown ups are not expected to go to kindergarten schools. They should only go to higher standards. This does not mean that they should pull down the kindergarden schools. On the other hand they should build more schools to serve more pupils. The great Tamil saint and poetess Avvai said, "Do not fix your habitation in a place where there is no temple." This she said as an ethical precept. The Tamil expression used by her for the temple is 'Koyil' which means house of God. Her precept is a universal precept which should be followed by one and all irrespective of religious affiliations. Adi Shankara had a lower deck in the vehicle of his teaching. He tolerated the worship of five chosen Deities, viz.

(1) Shiva (2) Vishnu (3) Surya (4) Ambal (5) Ganesha by all those who have not reached the standard required for travel in the upper deck of his philosophy.

Many Hindus with ulterior motives have painted Shankara as a rank idolater. This is a great injustice to him. Shankara has made his stand clear in the following verse composed by him.

> "Rupam rupa Vivargithasya bhavathe dhyanena yakalpitham
> Sthuthyanirvachaniyathakhilaguro durikritha yanmaya
> Vyapithawanja nirakritham bhagavatho yathirthayathradina
> Kshanthavyam jagadisa thatyukalatha doshthrayam mathkritham"

The meaning of the above is as follows:

I committed my first Sin Oh Lord of the Universe, by ascribing form to the formless; Praising with laudation that which is indescribable, I committed my second sin; Locating in a particular temple and locality the great Lord of the Universe, I committed my third sin; Oh Lord of the Universe pardon me for the triple sin.

The note of attrition contained in the above verse should be taken as a guide line by all in the study of Shankara and his philosophy. This is in consonance with the ancient vedantic philosophy. A similar verse of attrition is also found in the Avadutha Gita of Dattatreya which is produced below:

> "Tvad-yatraya vyapakata hata te
> Dyanena Chetah-parata hata te
> Stutya maya vak-parata hata te
> Kshmasva nityam trividhaparadhan"

Meaning, by my making pilgrimage to thee thy all-pervasiveness has been destroyed by me; with my meditations thy transcendance of the mind has been destroyed by me; By my singing thy praise thy transcendence of speech has been destroyed be me; forgive me these three sins.

Regarding the worship of Ganesha we have seen that he is popular with all cults and sects within the Hindu fold. He is worshipped in two forms. One is in his abstract ideal form. The other is in his concrete idol form. The worship of his idol form is done by ritualistic methods. It all depends upon the faith of the worshippers. Bereft of faith he still survives as a curio, attracting the attention of such people who have no faith in him.

GANESHA AND HIS MARTYRDOM

Man is said to be a rational being for the reason that he can employ reason in all matters connected with his existence. This process of reasoning is called rationalism which is originally understood in a limited sense as the practice of explaining the supernatural in religion in a way consonant with reason or of treating reason as the ultimate authority in religion. Rationalism has a wider approach. Lord Buddha employed reason in propounding his law. He says in the Kalama Sutta "Do not believe in what you have heard; do not believe in traditions because they have been handed down for many generations; do not believe in anything because it is rumoured and spoken by many; do not believe merely because the written statement of some old sage is produced; do not believe in conjectures; do not believe in that as truth to which you have become attached by habit; do not believe merely on the authority of your teachers and elders. After observation and analysis when it agrees with reason and is conducive to the good and benefit of one and all,then accept it and live upto it."

Yogavashishta also says, that rational investigation is an important step in acquiring knowledge. Rational investigation really aims at realism and it is equally employed in matters other than religion, like physics, metaphysics, psychology and other realms of thought where reasoning is required. It is by employment of reason that people try to understand the nature of God. Truth and Morality. But these three matters have so far eluded their grasp. The nature of God is still in speculation and the standard of truth and morality appear to be relative.

In spite of this hapless situation rationalism continues its appeal to all those who have cultivated thinking habits and who rebel against the social and religious inequities perpetuated by long habits of restricted thinking. These free thinkers cannot be silent spectators of the inhuman atrocities perpetrated in society in the name of religion and tradition. Can any one subscribe to the inhuman atrocities of torture on nonviolent Jain monks by putting them on spikes by Hindus and torturing Christians by thumb screws, collar of torture and burning them alive by their co-religionists during medieval times? Similarly can any self respecting individual tolerate slavery and bonded labour in society without registering a protest? Free thinking movement is a natural reaction to such atrocities committed by man against man in the name of God and his religion.

As an ideal the movement is excellent provided the ways and means adopted to achieve the desired results are peaceful. Buddha, Mahavira, Shankara, Ramanuja, Nanak, Kabir, Mahatma Gandhi and a host of others were rationalists and reformers in their own way. They always adopted peaceful methods.

When free thinking degenerates to licensed thinking, rationalism degenerates into sententious individualism or groupism, This is the starting point of intolerance and fanaticism. Fanatic rationalism is as dangerous as fanatic religiosity. In ordinary hands fanatic rationalism ends in violence, bloodshed and chaos.

Genesha fell a victim to this sort of fanatic rationalism. In the past we had in India Charvakas and Lokayatas. They were more materliastic than rationalistic in their outlook. They left Ganesha unmolested. The present Century saw the reactions of the sins of the past committed by man against man in the name of God and his religion. Quite a number of free thinkers came forward to reform religion and society in the light of their own understanding, Ganesha being a Hindu Deity with precedence over all other Deities attracted the attention of these zealous men. They have seen contemporary politicians burning the effigies of their opponents to give vent to their feelings. A similar strategy was adopted and they decided to inaugurate a campaign by smashing this funny God out of existence and demonstrate to the masses the Gods' impotency in averting this disaster. In pursuance of this decision, these enthusiastic men procured a huge idol of Ganesha with profane make ups and took it in procession to a public place where the members of the public could see for themselves the God's helplessness against his own fate. The planning was done so precisely that at the appointed time Ganesha was smashed to pieces within the sight of his helpless devotees.

Mohamed Gazani and Mohamed Ghori broke idols of Gods for the love of loot. But these free thinkers broke the idol of Ganesha as a master strategy for the reformation of the society and its religion. But they did not achieve the expected results. The strategy misfired.

The removal of caste distinction and superstition is laudable. But where is the question of superstition and caste in the matter of Ganesha? He is a symbol Deity moulded by the God essence in man and he could be discerned only by the same faculty. A mahavakya (Great saying) says 'Na Devo Devam Archayat" meaning one cannot venerate God unless one is God himself. Ganesha was originally a Sudra Devatha. Now he has also become a Brahmin Devatha. The smashing of Ganesha in public has done more harm to free thinking and rationalism than to Ganesha. So far as Ganesha is concerned it is his martyrdom and he has resurrected like Phoenix with more vigour. It may be noted, that this vigour of Ganesha is imparted to him by the faith of his devotees. Faith like love is a higher quality of mind. But blind faith like blind love may not lead one to the desirable end. Faith in images and their worship should be kept within strict limits and knowledgeable people and spiritual heads should constantly remind people that the image is after all only a symbol of God without meaning any disrespect either to the image or its worshippers. It is said that when Khalif Umar expressed doubts about the Black stone in Kaba and its ceremonial kissing

Lord Ganesha at R.K. Studios, Bombay – 1991

Marble Ganesha dancing pose made at Jaipur from Macrana marble & with Glow painting

by muslim pilgrims, Hazarat Ali explained to him "Al hajru Yamin-ullah-f-il-Ard" meaning this stone is as God's right hand on earth.

Ganesha is not a mere piece of stone like the black stone of Kaba. As already indicated he is a Deity shaped by the sublime qualities of human nature. This Deity has acquired a sanctity that even the Mugal Emperor Aurangazeb is said to have made liberal endowments to the Ganesha Temple at Chinchawada near Poona.

Let us therefore sing Alleluia to Ganesha.

Shri Mayureshwar – Morgaon

GANESHA AND MYTHOLOGY

 *Prof.* Max Mueller said that mythology is a disease of language and that ancient symbolism was the result of something like primitive aberration of mind. There may be many who may subscribe to this view of Prof. Max Mueller. But a good many may also share the view of Prof. Mircea Elaide who said that images, symbols and myths are not irresponsible creatures of the psyche and that they resound to a need and fulfill a function there of bringing to light the most hidden modalities of being.

Prof. Mircea Elaide spoke both as a scholar and as a mystic while Prof. Max Mueller spoke only as a great scholar that he was.

Mythology is a primitive mode of expressing thoughts based on natural facts. There cannot be any aberration in this mode of collecting thoughts. For example, the ancient Egyptians described the mouse as an external symbol of the soul. The soul is something residing within our body and it is compared with a mouse which lives underground in its burrow unseen by anybody. Similarly ancient Egyptians, also considered cat as the symbol of the moon for the reason that the eye of the car can see in the darkness and it reflects light that falls on it just like the moon reflects the light of the Sun.

The Hindu Puranas, the mosaic and Christian treatment, ancient Sumarian and Egyptian lore are full of myths containing symbols, emblems, allegories and parables, which are resorted to by masterminds, as they are the best medium to bring home to popular minds the meaning behind abstract ideas and concepts. Revelations of St. John the divine is full of such symbols and allegories. Song of Solomon, Rasleela stories of Radha and Krishna and the legend of Laila and Majnu are also writings of a legendary nature depicting the yearning of the worshipper to get merged with the worshipped. These writings are made deliberately interesting, by a down to earth approach, with a platonic ideal underlying them. There are, in like manner many stories about Ganesha. Some stories are silly. Some stories are serious. The most popular one among these stories is the one regarding his birth, as the mind born son of the Goddess Parvathy, his exploits, decapitation and resurrection.

Succinctly started the story is as follows:

Parvathy the great Goddess annoyed at the too many intrusions of her consort Shiva, into her private apartments in her palace at Kailas posted the bull headed Nandi an attendant of Shiva at the gate with strict instructions not to let any body in, without her permission. A little later Shiva came there but Nandi not being bold enough to prevent the entry of his master, let him in. Parvathy though courteous to her Lord was furious at Nandi for violating her instructions. Shiva got amused at her annoyance and left the place to allow things to settle down. Parvathy decided to have her own attendant who could obey her orders, come what may. She collected all the scented unguent from her body and by will of her own mind created a boy. She looked at him and was pleased to see him strong and handsome. She hugged him as her own son and presenting him with a staff posted him at her palace gate with instructions to let no one in without her permission. A few moments later Shiva came at the gate with his attendants and attempted to get in. The boy cried halt. Shiva got furious at the effrontery of the boy and pushed him out of his way. The boy dealt a heavy blow on Shiva with his staff and the situation become very awkward. Shiva's attendants also were bewildered. Shiva on second thought decided to leave the place discreetly instructing his attendants to remove the impudent boy standing guard at the gate.

After Shiva left the place his attendants headed by Nandi made several attacks on the boy who with his staff repulsed every attack and finally put them all to flight. Brahma, Vishnu and Indra who knew about this commotion at the palace gate of Parvathy wanted to prevent any estrangement between Shiva and Parvathy which would affect the entire universe. They hastened to Shiva and offered their humble services as mediators between him and his consort. Shiva accepting their offer asked Brahma first to go to the boy standing guard at the gate and put some sense into his head. Brahma went to the boy but found him adamant. The boy told Brahma that he would not allow any one in, not even Shiva, without his mother's permission.

The situation grew worse. Shiva summoned his son Karthikeya and held consultations with him as also with Brahma, Vishnu and Indra. They decided to remove the boy by force and mustered before the palace gate. Parvathy gauged the situation and created two furies in the nature of Deities by name Kali and Durga to help the boy.

There was a great melee at the gate. The boy was helped by Kali and Durga and Shiva was helped by the other gods and his own attendants. The boy was invincible in a straight fight. So Shiva decided to kill the boy by an attack from behind. In this attack from behind Shiva severed the head of the boy. The situation which was confused got worse confounded. Parvathy decried this act of cowardice on the part of her consort. Shiva realising the mistake began to repent. Brahma and Vishnu approached Parvathy for a solution and Parvathy dictated

that the boy should be brought back to life and that the resurrected boy should be made a Deity and given precedence in the pantheon of Gods. She also hinted that if this is not done, she would herself start fighting to retrieve the situation.

Shiva was appraised of the terms of truce. He did not want

any further confrontation with Parvathy. So he advised Brahma and Vishnu to go towards North and bring the head of the first being they would meet. They did as they were told and met an elephant with a single tusk. Vishnu cut its head with his discus and brought it to Shiva and Shiva asked Brahma to transplant it on the headless body of the boy. This was done and the boy came to life again with the head of the elephant. There was all round jubilation. Shiva and Parvathy were reconciled. Shiva made the resurrected boy as the leader of his retinue and gave him the title of Vigneshwara (Lord in control of all obstacles). After this investiture, it has become a practice that Ganesha's blessings are first invoked by one and all before any ceremony is begun.

Although Ganesha was created without the intervention of Shiva, after his resurrection with the head of the elephant Shiva also took pride about the part played by him in his resurrection and recognised him as his elder son. It may be noted that Ganesha had already come into existence before Karthikeya was created by Shiva without the intervention of Parvathy.

The above legend may read like an exaggerated account of a bickering between a Hindu Goddess and her spouse. But there is in it a wealth of spiritual information which may elude a casual reader or a sneering critic.

We have said that Ganesha is a prevedic Deity. In the prevedic period the society was matriarchal when people worshipped a Magna Mater symbolised and called in India by several names like Avvai, Ayi, Mayi, Maya, Ambal and by thousands of other names of which Parvathy is also one.

Before the Prophet of Islam became a monotheist about the middle of his life, Arabs also were worshipping the Magna Mater under different names like Al Umma, Al Uza, Al Lat and Al Manat besides the male Deity Shiva. The matriarchal system was the order of the society in Arabia and other neighbouring countries. In the early days of Christianity the "Holy Ghost" was considered as a mother. It is stated in one of the Apocryphas that Christ himself has spoken of "My Mother the Holy Ghost."

Baha-ulla a muslim reformist of nineteenth Century and the founder of Bahai faith speaks of the great Magna Mater as the "Luminous Maid of Heavens" clad in white, who comforted him when he was languishing in the prison of Nazir-U-Din Sha, with the weight of a heavy iron collar round his neck.

It is this mother conception of God that is personified and called Parvathy, the mother of Ganesha. She is a matrix of the world besides being the mother of

Ganesha. The conception of God as a male and as father of all creations came into vogue at a later date as was the case with Judaism. Even in the above mentioned legend, Shiva does not count much in the presence of Parvathy and her son, Ganesha. The role of Indra, Brahma and Vishnu the three vedic Gods as peace makers indicates the beginning of the fusion of vedic

and prevedic cultures. The vedic God Rudra had been merged with Shiva. But even with this added strength, he was unable to override the prevedic Goddess represented in the legend as Parvathy.

Although God is sexless the transition from mother conception to father conception depended upon the importance given to the father in the society. Judaism and Islam gave importance to father but Christianity while recognising God as father gave importance to the son who was the son of Holy Mary, the great mother. Whatever may be the doctrinaire differences between Ganesha cult of the Hindus and other religious cults, the fact remains that Ganesha is the son of his mother begotten by her without reference to a father. This aspect of Ganesha though abstract is in tune with the theory of immaculate conception propounded by many religions.

 Parvathy stands as the generative force. The annihilation of the impetuous, obstinate and belligerent boy by Shiva is for the transformation of the boy into a calm, reasonable and purposeful being. Shiva is the lord of yoga and the fixing of the head of the slaughtered elephant with one tusk on to the trunk of the boy is symbolical of the transformation of the boy into a spiritual being. For securing the head of the elephant Shiva asked Brahma and Vishnu to go to the North (utharam). The journey to the North is the Devayana or Savya path of enlightenment. This head of the elephant which they brought had only one tusk which is indicative of the nondualistic aspect of the mind after enlightenment, the result of the journey to the North. The bull-headed Nandi figuring as the major — domo of Shiva's house-hold in the story, is a character that cannot be dismissed without a thought for the reason that he enjoys the confidence of both Shiva and Parvathy. Nandy is a symbol of the psychic light seen by the students of yoga inside the brow region. The name Nandi is a corruption of the compound word "Nuthal-thie" containing two concepts, viz. 'Nuthal' meaning brow and 'Thie' meaning fire or light. "Nuthal-thie" therefore refers to the psychic light seen inside the brow region. Shiva is the life principle or the God within us and it is in the wake of this psychic illumination that the yogi realises that Nandi is the approach to Shiva.

Thus the legend of Ganesha is not a tale of absurdities. There are several other stories about him and each one appears to have been designed to throw some light on any one or more of his spiritual aspects. Deciphering these stories is as difficult as deciphering the inner meanings of the several symbols and expressions given in the revelations of St. John the Divine.

To understand the inner meanings of all mythological stories and mystic symbols connected with any religion one should rise above all morbid sectarianism and mental myosis and inhibitions. The observation of Pope John XXIII is worth emulation. "Men do not understand each other. Religions quarrel among themselves because they do not understand the religion at its best. Divisions and quarrels in the name of religion are on the surface like waves in the sea. But deeper you fathom religion, you get to unity, universality, and catholicity." It is in the light of this papal aphorism that one should study Ganesha in all his aspects.

In Chapter Four, we have noted that Shiva energised by Agni, incognito as a mouse originated Karthikeya who stands in relationship to Ganesha as a brother. In this study of Ganesha, it is worthwhile to know something about this brother. The next chapter deals with Karthikeya.

Shri Varadvinayak – Mahad

Ganesha in Lights

Engrav'd by J. Swaine

ꦲꦴꦗꦸꦛ ꦤꦴꦩꦴ

Bitára Gána — or Ganésa

From a Subject in Stone brought from Sing á sári.

London, Published by Black, Parbury & Allen, Leadenhall Street, 1817

100 year old rare picture

GANESHA AND KARTHIKEYA

*I*n the previous chapter we have dealt with the origin, growth and metamorphosis of Ganesha as mentioned in the Hindu mythology. Obviously, Ganesha started life in matriarchal prevedic society and was not recognised by the patriarchal vedic society. His brother Karthikeya known by several names like Kumara, Subramanya, Skanda, Shanmugha was recognised by the vedic society. He is identified as Sanath Kumar, the mind born son of Brahma at a time when Brahma was considered as a supreme Deity. When Shiva became the supreme Deity Karthikeya became the mind born son of Shiva. He is described as the commander-in-chief of the army of Devas who destroyed the demons, Tharakasura, Surapadma and Simhamukha, the arch enemies of both mankind and Devas.

Like Ganesha, Karthikeya is also a personification of a metaphysical concept. In South India he is called Subramanya (Resplendent light) which is the same as the Huq Nur of the Sufis symbolising divine wisdom. The name Karthikeya is associated with Karthika (Pleiades) group of stars in which one could pick up six faintly glowing stars. According to Greek mythology, King Atlas has seven daughters. Of these, one married a mortal and so lost a bit of her brilliance and became invisible. There are several other stars in the group which can be detected only by a powerful telescope. Alceone is the brightest star in this group. It is said that our Sun which gives us energy to sustain our life is controlled by Alceone and that is the reason why the entire group of Pleaides stars is called Karthika meaning creative force, and Karthikeya is a personification of this force.

According to Hindu mythology, the six stars visible to the naked eye are considered to be the six celestial virgins who had a simultaneous and immaculate conception through the grace of Shiva. These virgins consolidated their gain and brought forth a divine child.

The child was named Karthikeya as he was born of the six Karthika virgins. Karthika as above mentioned is to be taken as the symbol of the creative power of Shiva and Karthikeya stands in the father and son relationship with Shiva which relationship Ganesha cannot claim for the reason that he was created by Parvathy by power of her Will.

Karthikeya rides a peacock and is more airborne like Vishnu on his Garuda (the kite with white breast) and Brahma on his Hamsa (the white swan). His association is more with Devas and he is not within each reach of one and all whether mortal or immortal. Ganesha on the other hand rides a mouse and is more earth bound and within easy reach of one and all. This accounts for his popularity.

Although Karthikeya, is a vedic Deity and was popular among the people of Aryavartha, his popularity waned there and he had to migrate to the South and occupy the shrines built for him on hill tops. The most famous among these shrines in South India is the one situated on the top of Palani Hill. Karthikeya is called as Subramanya in the Palani Shrine. We have noted that Subrmanya conveys the same meaning as Huq Nur of the Sufis. It is significant that in this shrine there is also a nirvikalpa samathi (tomb) of Saint Bogar who equated Allah with Shiva as could be gleaned from a collection of his mystic verses in Tamil known by the name of "Bogar Seven Thousand." Evidently Bogar like Vavar of Sabarimalai was a sufi saint. It is said that he himself constructed the shrine for the sake of his Hindu and Muslim disciples. Even at the present time both communities offer worship there, the Hindus facing the idol and Muslims avoiding the idol. Many miracles are said to be taking place at the shrine.

Subramanya is also called his devotees as 'Palani Andi' (the Faquir of Palani). He is referred to by the great Tamil mystic poet Sri Arunagirinathar as 'Venjur Konra Ravuthar (the Muslim hero who killed the horrible demon Sura) and Kalapa Mayil Erum Ravuthar (the Muslim hero who rides the peacock with splendid tail). Subramanya's association with peacock is mentioned by Sufis metaphorically as Nuri Mohammed (the lustrous Mohammed) becoming manifest in peacock and perching on the top of the tree of assurance singing songs in praise of God prostrating five times in prayer. The peacock is considered as a sacred bird not only by the Hindus but also by the Muslims of Sufi order. The peacock has now become a national bird of India and is given protection by operation of law.

There is also a Ganesha idol at the Palani Shrine. But it is situated outside the sanctum sanctorum for the obvious reason that he should be the one to be propitiated first, by the pilgrims who visit the shrine.

Although Karthikeya was not included in the Panchayatnana concession of worship by Adi Shankara, his name appears to have been subsequently added to make the list contain six Deities known by the composite name of Shanmatham meaning worship of six Deities, viz. Shiva, Vishnu, Sun, Ambal, Ganesha and Subramanya. Karthikeya and Ganesha maintain good fraternal relationship although now and then Ganesha is seen up to some prank with his brother. A dispute arose between the brothers as to who should get married first. They approached their parents for a decision. The parents decided that the one who goes round the world and comes first would be the one to get married first.

This was accepted by the brothers as reasonable. Karthikeya mounted his aerial vehicle the peacock and started on his journey. As soon as he was out of sight, Ganesha mounted his mouse and went round Shiva and explained his action as tantamount to going round the world as Shiva himself is the embodiment of the world being its creator. Subramanya after

completing his journey came late and was chagrined to find that Ganesha had outwitted him.

Such stories though meant to cater to the vulgar fancies, show how much backing Ganesha is getting so as to get an edge over his brother in the Hindu Pantheon. Karthikeya wielded a lance and fought the enemies of mankind whereas Ganesha wielded a stylo and acted as a scribe to Krishna Badarayana (Vedavyasa) and preserved the sacred teachings of Hindus for the benefit of posterity, according to puranic accounts.

Shri Chintamani – Theur

GANESHA AND HIS FESTIVAL

We have noted that Ganesha is also known as Vinayaka which means that he is considered as the lord of the Holy Breath of Life and that this Holy Breath of life is different from the air of the atmosphere. We have also noted that medulla oblongata situated above the throat region controls the breathing process which is the first among the bodily functions of Prana and that this organ can be identified as the Muladharam. Ganesha being the presiding Deity of this psychic centre, he should be considered as the personification of the psychic forces within us which could be evoked for spiritual elevation. We have also noted that the practice of yoga is the best method to stimulate the psychic centres. But this method requires great mental discipline and rectitude. In fact only very few people follow this method in the honest way.

In the practice of religion most people follow the path if ritualism. For people who have adopted the ethics of yama and niyama, ritualism may be a slow acting method of stimulating the psychic centres. Ritualism done with personal devotion is an appeal to the psyche in the individual. When demonstrated in a festive manner with a group appeal it becomes a festival. The several devotees, who whether with devotion or without devotion participate in the festival and even onlookers are caught in the elation and joy of the occasion. In festival, the appeal is to the psyche in the mass. But in any case ritualism bereft of the ethics of yama and niyama will not bring about any spiritual advancement.

The most important festival connected with Ganesha is the vinayaka chathurthi. In this festival, Ganesha is invoked as the lord of the breath of life indicated by his name Vinayaka. This festival falls on the fourth day of the new moon in the month of Simha or shravana (August-September). According to the Hindu calendar each of the twelve divisions of the zodiac corresponds to a month each month being governed by its own tutelary planet. The month Simha, is governed by the Sun the lord of our solar system. Esotèrically Sun is the symbol of the soul even in astrology and moon is the symbol of the mind.

When the moon in the course of its transit occupies any division where the sun also appears to be transitting the phenomenon of the New Moon appears. Esoterically this phenomenon is taken as the symbol of the merger of the mind with the soul. All desires of the mind are resolved in this blackout of perfect sunyam or emptiness. The state of sunyam is different from the state of nothingness. It is the state of absolute existence. It is not a negative notion. Dr. Jung calls this state as pleroma which is both full and empty. This state of existence is called in simple language as amohavasam (a life bereft of all desires). That is why the new moon is called amavasi which is a corruption of amohavasam. It is because of this esoteric significance orthodox Hindus consider amavasi as an auspicious day.

Amavasi state of mind is just like the mind of the foetus in the womb. Only after it comes out into the world it begins to express itself in terms of Manam (mind), Chith (Sub-conscious state), Buddhi (intellect) and Ahamkaram (ego). It is the ego the last stage of prana's manifestation that sustains the phenomenal world of relative values and it is this ego that is responsible for all the travails of life. This stage of ego is symbolised as the fourth day from Amavasi (New Moon) in the month of Simha and celebrated as Vinayaka Chathurthi. Amavasi to Pournami (Full Moon) is a waxing cycle of the ego projected from the mind, culminating in pournami. In pournami, the sun and moon are in opposition. Though pournami has a halo of poetic fancy, it has an imperceptible power to excite and make people run berserk.

From this culmination point of pournami where the ego is at the height of its conceit, there begins another warning cycle. In this waning phase the orbe of the moon gets diminished every day and finally disappears in the darkness of amavasi. This amavasi (new moon) coming after Vinayaka Chathurthi is a more meaningful festival called Mahalaya amavasi which means the great merger of the mind with soul, bereft of all desires. Maha means the great and laya means the spiritual merger of the mind with the soul. Mahalaya amavasi should be considered as a symbol of spiritual progress of the devotee or sadhaka. The next nine days are observed by Hindus as holy days. They go by the name of Navaratri during which people are expected to worship Saraswathi Goddess of wisdom either by contemplative practice or by ritualism. The tenth day is the symbol day of victory of wisdom over ignorance and celebrated with great joy and enthusiasm. This tenth day is called "Vijaya dasami" (The victorious tenth day).

The Amavasi preceding Vinayaka chathurthi and the Mahalaya amavasi, together form a base for a higher spiritual point synchronising with the next Amavasi day. This is the Deepavali amavasi a symbol day of luminous wisdom which is celebrated as a festival of lights. The dark forces of hell symbolised as Narakasura (Demon of the hell) are dispelled and the mind becomes happy in its own illumination. These three amavasi days constitute a triangle, the base laying between the amavasi preceding Vinayaka chathurthi and Mahalaya amavasi and the apex lying at the Deepavali amavasi. This imaginary triangle is the symbol of shaktipitam (seat of divine energy) and that is the reason why Sakthi the great mother of the universe is called Thrikonika. Her other name is Ganamba, the mother of Ganesha. We have seen that Vinayaka chathurthi a festival connected with Ganesha is followed by a number of other festivals. Ganesha being the inaugurating Deity, his part cannot be underestimated. During this festival of Vinayaka chathurthi people make his image in clay and after all the ritualistic worship and other religious formalities are over, they are thrown in water. This destruction has an esoteric significance.

Ganesha's clay image signifies the Prithvi Thathvam. Prithvi is one of the five mahabuthas and a repository of senses of sabda, sparsa, rupa, resa and gandha. Throwing the Ganesha images in water and disintegrating them is symbolical of the disintegration of the mind from the objects of senses and enlightening it to merit higher spiritual elevations indicated by Mahalaya amavasi, Navaratri, Vijaya dasami and Deepavali festivals.

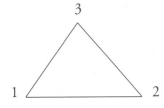

(1) Amavasi preceeding Vinayaka chathurthi

(2) Mahalaya amavasi

(3) Deepavali amavasi

Shree Siddhi Vinayak – Bombay

From the Art Gallery

SHREE GANESH ATHARVA SHEERSHA

Om Shree Ganeshaya Namaha

In the Name of Lord Ganesh, we start our reading of "Ganapati Atharvashirsa". Atharvan Rishi, who has had the "darshan" — the direct experience of Lord Ganesha, has conveyed these in poetic form, so that we can benefit from it.

It is customary to invoke the name of Lord Ganesha before beginning anything. Atharvan rishi states:

Hari Om Namaste Ganapataye
Tvameva Prathyaksham Tatvamasi
Tvameva Kevalam Kartasi
Tvameva Kevalam Dhartasi
Tvameva Kevalam Hartasi
Tvameva Sarvam Khalvidam Bramhasi
Tvameva Shaksad Atmasi Nityam || 1 ||

O! Lord Ganesha
I pay my deep homage to you,
The lord of the deva-gana
you are the first facet
of the Brahma-Tatva to arise
You have alone created this entire universe
You alone can maintain this universe
You alone can destroy this universe
You are indeed the all conquering supreme Lord
Indeed you are the 'Atma' (of this Cosmos). || 1 ||

Hrtum Vachmi
Satyam Vachmi || 2 ||
I speak noble fact
I speak the complete truth || 2 ||

Ava Tvam Mam Ava vaktaram
Ava Shrotaram Ava Dataram
Ava Dhataram Avanu Chanmav Shishyam
Ava Paschatat Ava Purastat
Avo Utharatat Ava Dakshinatat
Avachodarvatat Ava Dharatat
Sarvatomam Pahi Pahi Samamtat || 3 ||

Protect me
Protect the one who describes you
Protect all who hear about your characteristics

Protect me & the ones who worship you
Protect all disciples who are under Tutelege
Protect me from the obstacles
(which arise during rituals) from the East
(similarly) protect me from the West, North, and South

Protect me from above & below
Protect me from all directions || 3 ||

Tvam Vangamyatsvam Chinmaya
Tvam Anandmayatsvam Bramhamaya
Tvam Satchitananda Dvitiyosi
Tvam Pratyaksam bramhasi
Tvam Jnanamayo Vijnanamayoasi || 4 ||

You are the constituent of speech
You are joy & immortal consciousness
You are truth, mind & bliss —
One without a second
You are none other than divinity
You are knowledge of gross & subtle types || 4 ||

Sarvam Jagadidam Tatvato Jayate
Sarvam Jagadidam Tvatsti Shastati
Sarvam Jagadidam Tvayi Layamesyati
Sarvam Jagadidam Tvayi Pratyeti
Tvam Bhumi Rapo Nalo Nilo Nabha
Tvam Chatvarim vak padini || 5 ||

All the universes manifest due to you
All the universes are sustained by you
All the universes get destroyed in you
All the universes finally get merged in you
You alone are earth, water, fire, air & ether
You are the 4 types of speech & the root source of sound || 5 ||

Tvam Guna Traya Atitaha;
Tvam Avastreya Atitaha
Tvam Deha Treya atitaha
Tvam Kala Treya atitaha
Tvam Muladhar Stiti yosi Nityam
Tvam Shakti treya atmak
Tvam yogino dhyayanti nityam
Tam Bramha, Tvam Vishnustvam,
Rudrastvam, Indrastvam, Agnistvam, Vayustvam, Suryastvam, chandramastvam,
bramha bhur bhuva svorom || 6 ||

You are beyond the 3 "Gunas" (Satva; Pure, Rajas;
Activating & Tamas; Dull);
You are beyond the 3 states of being; (Awake, Dream &
Deep Sleep)
You are beyond the bodies; (Gross, subtle & Casual);
You are beyond past, present & future
You always reside in the "Muladhara" chakra
You are the trinity of power, (creative, maintaining & destructive powers) sages
always meditate on you
You are the creator, sustainer, destroyer, the lord of 3 worlds, fire, air, sun, moon,
you are all inclusive & all pervading.

Ganadim Purvamuccharya Varnadim Tadanantaram
Anusvara paratarah ardhendu lasitam taren hridam etatva manu svarupam
gakarah purva rupam akaro madhyam rupam
Anu svaraschanta rupam bindu ruta rupam
Nadah sandhanam sa hita sandhih sesha ganeshvidya ganak rishih: nichrud
gayatri chandah ganpatir devata
"Om gung" Ganapataye namaha || 7 ||
(After describing the characteristics & cosmic attributes of Lord Ganesha,
atharvan rishi gives us the sacred "Ganesh Vidya" i.e. the mantra which reveals
the sacred form of Lord Ganesh).
The Letter "Ga" is to be enunciated, followed by "Na". This one word mantra is
then potentiated with the "pranava" "Om". This is sacred mantra.
In order to make it simpler, atharvan rishi presents the above in an easier fashion.
Remember that knowledge was transmitted orally in those days).In the first part
'Na' is the middle & end. The 'UM' formed by the bindu is conjoined with the
foregoing & all of them from the sacred word. This mantra if pronounced
properly, has the power of revealing the divine lord Ganesh, the sage who receives
the mantra is Ganaka & the metre is "nichrat gayatri", the deity is Ganapati.
Om "Gung" Ganapati, my salutations to you || 7 ||
(Saying thus, the devotee should bow to the lord).

Ek Dantaya vid mahe, vakra tundaya dhimihi
Tanno danti prachodayat || 8 ||
I meditate on the single tusked lord, with his bent trunk
May he grant knowledge & inspire me
(This is the Ganesh "'Gayatri", which is self sufficient).

Eka dantam chatur hastam pashmam kusha dharinam
radam cha vardam hastair bhi bhranum mushaka dhvajam
Raktam lambodharam shoorpa karnkam rakta vasasam
Rakta Gandhanu liptangam rakta pushpaihi supujitam
Kmpinam devam jagat karnam achutam
avir bhutam cha shrasta yadao, prakrutehe purushat param evam dhyayati yo
nityam, sa yogi yoginam varah || 9 ||

(The "Saguna" form of Lord Ganesha is presented in the above shloka)
I salute the Lord with 1 tusk (right side) he has 4 hands;
upper right carrying binding rope; upper left holding goad;
The mouse on his banner is also his vehicle
He is blood red in colour; pot - bellied; he has elephant ears & wears red clothes
He is smeared with red sandalwood & decorated with red flowers
He is eternally blessing his devotees & was existing before the cosmos
He is beyond "Prakriti" & "Purusha" & is ever creating universes.
One who meditates on him constantly, is a supreme yogi || 9 ||

Namo Vrat Pataye, Namo Ganpataye Namh Pramat pataye, namaste stu
Lambodaraya ekadantaya, vighna nashine shiv sutaya, sri varad murtiye namo
namah || 10 ||

(Salutations to you) Lord of all deities, Ganas & all beings (salutations to) the
pot-bellied one with 1 tusk who destroys all obstacles, son of Shiva, the divine
lord who grants boons (we bow to you) taking your name || 10 ||

Hari om Namaste Ganapataye
Tvameva Pratyaksham Tatvamasi
Tvameva kevalam kartasi
Tvameva kevalam dhartasi
Tvameva kevalam hartasi
Tvameva sarvam khalvidam bramhasi
Tvameva shaksad atmasi nityam || 11 ||

O! Lord Ganesha
I pay my deep homage to you,
The lord of the Deva-Gana,
You are the first facet of the Bramha-tatva to arise you have lone created this
entire universe
You alone can maintain this universe
You alone can destroy this universe
You are indeed the all conquering supreme lord indeed you are the "Atma" (of
the cosmos) || 1 ||

GANESH SHASRANAM or 1000 NAMES OF LORD GANESHA

|| Shree Ganeshaya Namah
Shree Devi Saraswateya Namah
Shree Gurubhyu Namah ||

Om Ganeshwarai Namah
Om Gankridya Namah
Om Gannathaya Namah
Om Ganadhipaya Namah

Om Ekdrishtaya Namah
Om Vakratundaya Namah
Om Gajvakraya Namah
Om Mahodaraya Namah
Om Lambodaraya Namah
Om Dhumravaranaya Namah
Om Vikataya Namah
Om Vighnanayanakaya Namah
Om Sumukhaya Namah
Om Dumu Namah
Om Buddhaya Namah
Om Vighnarajaya Namah
Om Gajananaya Namah
Om Bhimaya Namah
Om Pramodaya Namah
Om Aanodaya Namah
Om Suranandaya Namah
Om Mohatkataya Namah
Om Herambhaya Namah
Om Shambaraya Namah
Om Shambhavey Namah
Om Lambakaranaya Namah
Om Mahabalaya Namah
Om Nandanaya Namah
Om Alampataya Namah
Om Abhirvey Namah
Om Meghnadaya Namah
Om Gangajaya Namah
Om Vinayakaya Namah
Om Virupakshaya Namah
Om Dhirshuraya Namah

Om Varpradaya Namah
Om Maha Ganpatye Namah
Om Buddhipriyaya Namah
Om Shipra Prasadnaya Namah
Om Rudra Priyaya Namah
Om Ganadhyakshaya Namah
Om Umaputraya Namah
Om Aaghnashaya Namah
Om Kumar Gurve Namah
Om Eshaan putraya Namah
Om Mushak Vahanaya Namah
Om Siddhi Priyaya Namah
Om Siddha Vinayakaya Namah
Om Avighaya Namah
Om Tumbarve Namah
Om Simhavahanaya Namah
Om Mohini Priyaya Namah
Om Katagkantaya Namah
Om Raj Putraya Namah
Om Shaalkaya Namah
Om Sammitaya Namah
Om Amitaya Namah
Om Kushma Mandsamsambhootye Namah
Om Durjaya Namah
Om Dhurjaya Namah
Om Jayaya Namah
Om Bhoopatye Namah
Om Bhoovanpatye Namah
Om Bhootnapatye Namah
Om Avyaya Namah
Om Vishwakatre Namah
Om Vishwa Mukhaya Namah
Om Vishwa Rupaya Namah
Om Nidhye Namah
Om Ghrunye Namah
Om Karye Namah
Om Kavina Mrushbhaya Namah
Om Bhramanaya Namah
Om Bhramanaspatye Namah

Om Jyeshta Rajaya Namah
Om Niddhi Patye Namah
Om Niddhi Priya Pati Priyaya Namah
Om Hiranmaya Puratanstaya Namah
Om Surya Mandal Madhya Gayay
   Namah
Om Karahatidhavsta Sindhu Salilaya
   Namah
Om Saamaghoshapriyaya Namah
Om Pushdantabhide Namah
Om Umangkelikutukine Namah
Om Muktidaya Namah
Om Kulpalnaya Namah
Om Kiritine Namah
Om Kundaline Namah
Om Harine Namah
Om vanmaline Namah
Om Manomayay Namah
Om Vymukhyahatdyatshriye Namah
Om Padahatijitshitye Namah
Om Sadhyojaatsvarnamujyamekline
   Namah
Om Dudirmithrite Namah
Om Duswapnahrite Namah
Om Prashanaya Namah
Om Gunine Namah
Om Nadapratisthitaya Namah
Om Surupaya Namah
Om Sarvanetradhivasaya Namah
Om Vivasana Shravaya Namah
Om Pitambaraya Namah
Om Khandardaya Namah
Om Khandendukrutshekharya Namah
Om Chitrangdashyamdashnaya Namah
Om Bhaalchandraya Namah
Om Chaturbhurjaya Namah
Om Yogadhipaya Namah
Om Tarkstaya Namah
Om Purshaya Namah
Om Gajakarnaya Namah
Om Ganadhirajaya Namah
Om Vijay Asthirajaya Namah
Om Gajpatidwajine Namah

Om Devdevaya Namah
Om Samarprandipkaya Namah
Om Vayukilkaya Namah
Om Vippaschidvardaya Namah
Om Nandonandbhihnaalahakaya
   Namah
Om Varahardanaya Namah
Om Mrityunjaya Namah
Om Vyaghrajinambaraya Namah
Om Ecchashaktidharya Namah
Om Devtrate Namah
Om Dyatavimardanaya Namah
Om Shambhuvakrodhyaya Namah
Om Shambhukopagne Namah
Om Shambhuhasyabhuve Namah
Om Shambhutejse Namah
Om Shivshokharine Namah
Om Guarisukhaya Namah
Om Umangmaljaya Namah
Om Gauri Tej Bhuve Namah
Om Swadhumibhavaya Namah
Om Yagna Kayaya Namah
Om Mahanadaya Namah
Om Girivashmarne Namah
Om Shubanaya Namah
Om Sarvaatmanye Namah
Om Sarvadevatmanye Namah
Om Brahma Murghane Namah
Om Kukupshrutye Namah
Om Brahmadkumbhaya Namah
Om Chily Ombhalaya Namah
Om Satyashiroruhaya Namah
Om Jaggazmadhloyameshnimeshaya
   Namah
Om Agneyakasomdrushe Namah
Om Girindrekardaya Namah
Om Gharmagharmeshtaya Namah
Om Sambruhithaya Namah
Om Grahatshardashnaya Namah
Om Vanijivhaya Namah
Om Vasavanasikaya Namah
Om Kulachalansaya Namah
Om Somakarghantaya Namah
Om Rudrashirogharaya Namah
Om Nadinandabhujaya Namah
Om Tarkansakaya Namah
Om Bhrumdhyasansthithkaraya
   Namah
Om Brahmavidyamadotkaya Namah

Om Vyomanabhaye Namah
Om Shrihridhaya Namah
Om Meru Prushtaya Namah
Om Arnavodaraya Namah
Om Prithvikatye Namah
Om Srishtilingaya Namah
Om Shelorve Namah
Om Dasrajaanokaya Namah
Om Pataljhangaya Namah
Om Munipadye Namah
Om Kalanghoshtaya Namah
Om Triyatnave Namah
Om Jyotirnarnda La Lalangulaya Namah
Om Hridayalanirshalaya Namah
Om Hripadmakarnikashalivi-yatkelisarovaraya Namah
Om Sadbhaktdhyanigadhaya Namah
Om Pujavarinivirtaya Namah
Om Pratapine Namah
Om Kashyapsutaya Namah
Om Ganpaya Namah
Om Vishtpine Namah
Om Baline Namah
Om Yashvasvine Namah
Om Dharmikaya Namah
Om Svojhase Namah
Om Prathmay Namah
Om Prathameshvaraya Namah
Om Chintamandivipatye Namah
Om Kalpadromvanalaya Namah
Om Ratnamandapamdhyastaya Namah
Om Ratna Sinha Shrayaya Namah
Om Trivashivodhrutpadaya Namah
Om Jwalini Maulilalitaya Namah
Om Nandananditpithshriye Namah
Om Bhogdabhushitasanaya Namah
Om Sakamdayinipithaya Namah
Om Sphurdugrasanashraya Namah
Om Tejovatishiroratnaya Namah
Om Satyanityavatisitaya Namah
Om Sarvavighanashinipithaya Namah
Om Sarvashaktayambijashraya Namah
Om Lipipadamasanadharaya Namah
Om Vanihadhamtrayashraya Namah
Om Unnataprapadaya Namah
Om Gudagulphaya Namah'

Om Savavrutpashirnkaya Namah
Om Pinjhangaya Namah
Om Shlishtajhhanve Namah
Om Sthulorve Namah
Om Pronmatkatye Namah
Om Nimnabhaye Namah
Om Sthoolkukshave Namah
Om Pinvakshase Namah
Om Brihutbhujaya Namah
Om Pinaskandaya Namah
Om Kambukantaya Namah
Om Lambovashtaya Namah
Om Lambanasikaya Namah
Om Bhagnavamardaya Namah
Om Tungasavyadantaya Namah
Om Mahahanve Namah
Om Hrasvanetratraya Namah
Om Shoorpakarnakaya Namah
Om Nibidmastkaya Namah
Om Stabkakaarkumbhagraya Namah
Om Ratnamaulye Namah
Om Nirangkushaya Namah
Om Sarpaharkatisutraya Namah
Om Sarpayagnopavitve Namah
Om Sarpakotirkataya Namah
Om Sarpagrevayakatangaya Namah
Om Sarpakakshodarabandhanaya Namah
Om Sarparajotariyakaya Namah
Om Raktaya Namah
Om Raktambdharaya Namah
Om Raktamalyavibhushaya Namah
Om Raktakshenaya Namah
Om Raktakaray Namah
Om Raktalvoshtapallavayaa Namah
Om Shvetaya Namah
Om Shvetambdharaya Namah
Om Shvetmalyavibhushnaya Namah
Om Shvetatpatraruchiraya Namah
Om Shvetchaamravijitaya Namah
Om Sarvanvayasampurnalakshna Namah
Om Sarvanbharanshobhadayalakshita Namah
Om Sarvashobhasamvitaya Namah
Om Sarvamangalmaanglaya Namah

Om Sarvakararnakarnaya Namah
Om Shangirne Namah
Om Bijapurine Namah
Om Gadadharya Namah
Om Ikshuchaapadharaya Namah
Om Shooline Namah
Om Chakrapanye Namah
Om Shrojbhrute Namah
Om Passhine Namah
Om Dhritdpalaya Namah
Om Shaalimanjaribhrute Namah
Om Svadantabhrute Namah
Om Kalpavallidharaya Namah
Om Vishwabhayadaikaraya Namah
Om Vashine Namah
Om Akshamaladharaya Namah
Om Nayan Mudravate Namah
Om Mudgarayaudhaya Namah
Om Purna Patrine Namah
Om Kambudharaya Namah
Om Vidhyutalisamudkaya Namah
Om Matrulingadharaya Namah
Om Kootharvatye Namah
Om Pushkar
    Stasvarnaghatipurnaratnabhi
    Varshakaya Namah
Om Bharati Sundari Nathaya Namah
Om Vinayakratipriyaya Namah
Om Mahalakshmi Priyatamaya Namah
Om Siddha Lakshmi Manoramaya
    Namah
Om Rama Ramesh Puruvangaya
    Namah
Om Dakshinomamaheswaraya Namah
Om Mahivaraha Vamangaya Namah
Om Rati Kandarpaschimaya Namah
Om Aamodamodjanaya Namah
Om Spramod Pramodanaya Namah
Om Samedhitsmrudhishriye Namah
Om Riddhi Siddhi Pravartkaya Namah
Om Dattasaumukhyasumukhaya
    Namah
Om Kantikandlitashraya Namah
Om Mandanavatyashritangrahye
    Namah
Om Krutdaumukhyadumurkhaya
    Namah
Om Vighnasampallvopghanya Namah
Om Sevonnidramadravyaya Namah

Om Vighnakrutighancharanaya Namah
Om Dravinishakti Satkrutaya Namah
Om Trivaprasanayanaya Namah
Om Jwalinipalinilekdhrushye Namah
Om Mohinimohanaya Namah
Om Bhogdayinikantimanditaya Namah
Om Kaminikantavakrashriye Namah
Om Adhishtavasundharaya Namah
Om Vasandharamdondhamahashang-
    nidhiprabhave Namah
Om Nanidsumatimaulimahapadmi-
    nidhiprabhave Namah
Om Sarva Sadguru Samnveyaya
    Namah
Om Shochiskeshahahridyashraya
    Namah
Om Eshaanmurghne Namah
Om Devendrashikhaye Namah
Om Pavanandaya Namah
Om Agrapratyegranayanaya Namah
Om Divyastranaprayogride Namah
Om Airavatadisvaarsha
    Varnavarnpriyaya Namah
Om Vjrayadastraparivaraya Namah
Om Ganachandasamashraya Namah
Om Jayajayparivaraya Namah
Om Vijayavijayavahaya Namah
Om Ajitachirtpadabjaya Namah
Om Nityanityawantsitaya Namah
Om Vilasinikrutlaasaya Namah
Om Shaundisaundaryamanditaya
    Namah
Om Anantaanantsukhdaya Namah
Om Sumangalsumangalaya Namah
Om Icchashaktiny
    Anshaktikriyashaktiniveshitaya
    Namah
Om Subhagashanshritpadaya Namah
Om Lalita Lalitashraya Namah
Om Kaminikamanaya Namah
Om Kammalini Kelilalatya Namah
Om Saraswatashraya Namah
Om Gaurinandanaya Namah

Om Shreeniketanaya Namah
Om Guru Guptapadaya Namah
Om Vachasiddhaya Namah
Om Vaghieshwaripatye Namah
Om Nalinikamykaya Namah
Om Vamramaya Namah
Om Jyesthmanormaya Namah
Om Raudrimudripadabjaya Namah
Om Humbijaya Namah
Om Tung Shaktikaya Namah
Om Vishwadijannatranaya Namah
Om Swahashakteye Namah
Om Sakilkaya Namah
Om Amritabidh Krutvasaya Namah
Om Maddhurnitlochanaya Namah
Om Uchistganaya Namah
Om Uchistganeshaya Namah
Om Gannayakaya Namah
Om Sarvakalikasansadhiye Namah
Om Nityashaivaya Namah
Om Digambaraya Namah
Om Aanpayaya Namah
Om Anantdrustaya Namah
Om Apremaya Namah
Om Ajramaraya Namah
Om Aanavilaya Namah
Om Apratiryaya Namah
Om Ahachutaya Namah
Om Amritay Namah
Om Aksharya Namah
Om Apratkaraya Namah
Om Akshayaya Namah
Om Ajaayaya Namah
Om Anadharaya Namah
Om Anaamyaya Namah
Om Amalaya Namah
Om Amoghsiddhye Namah
Om Advetaya Namah
Om Aghoraya Namah
Om Apramitanaya Namah
Om Ananakaraya Namah
Om Abdhibhoomy Agribalghnyaya Namah

Om Ayaktalakshanaya Namah
Om Adharpithaya Namah
Om Adharaya Namah
Om Adhar Radheya Varjitaya Namah
Om Aakhoketanaya Namah
Om Asha Purkaya Namah
Om Aakho Maha Rathaya Namah
Om Ikshu sagarmadhyastaya Namah
Om Ikshu Bhakshan Lalsaya Namah
Om Ikshuchaaptriekshriye Namah
Om Ikshuchaapnivesvitaya Namah
Om Indranil Samdhyutye Namah
Om Indivaradalshamaya Namah
Om Indumandalinirmalaya Namah
Om Indhmapriyaya Namah
Om Idabhagaya Namah
Om Iradhamne Namah
Om Indirapriyaya Namah
Om Ishwaku Vighna Vidhwanisne Namah
Om Itikartayatepistaya Namah
Om Ishaanmaulaye Namah
Om Ishaanaye Namah
Om Ishaanutaya Namah
Om Itighne Namah
Om Ishnatraya Kalpantay Namah
Om Ihamatra vivarjitaya Namah
Om Upendraya Namah
Om Uddabhrunmaulaye Namah
Om Underkablipriyaya Namah
Om Unnatannaya Namah
Om Uttungaya Namah
Om Udarravidashargrane Namah
Om Urjswate Namah
Om Ushmamalamdaya Namah
Om Ushapohadurasdaya Namah
Om Ridhisiddhipradaykay Namah
Om Rintraya Vimochkaya Namah
Om Lupta Vighnayasavabhaktana Namah
Om Lupta Shaktaya Surdvisha Namah
Om Lupta Visphot Nashanaya Namah
Om Ekar Pitha Madhyasaya Namah
Om Ekpaadkrutasmaya Namah
Om Ejitakhildyatshriye Namah
Om Edhitakhilamsshreyaya Namah
Om Aishwariam Nidhye Namah
Om Aishwaryaya Namah
Om Ehikamushkimpradaya Namah

....89

Om Erambhdasmunmeshaya Namah
Om Erawatnibhannaya Namah
Om Omkar Vachaya Namah
Om Omkaraya Namah
Om Ojaswate Namah
Om Oshdhipatye Namah
Om Audaryanidhye Namah
Om Aaudyatdhuraya Namah
Om Aaunatyaniswanaya Namah
Om Ankushayasuragana Namah
Om Ankushayasurvidhvisham Namah
Om Aamast Visargantpadeshoo-
    parikrititaya Namah
Om Kamandaloodharaya Namah
Om Kalpaya Namah
Om Karpadane Namah
Om Kalbhannaya Namah
Om Karmashakshine Namah
Om Karmakartye Namah
Om Karma Karmaphalpradya Namah
Om Kadamgolkakaraya Namah
Om Kushmandgannayakaya Namah
Om Karunyadhehaya Namah
Om Kapilaya Namah
Om Kaykaya Namah
Om Katisutrabhoote Namah
Om Sarvaya Namah
Om Khadagapriyaya Namah
Om Khadagkhantantasaya Namah
Om Khanimarlaya Namah
Om Khalvaatshrungnilayaya Namah
Om Khatvanghine Namah
Om Khadurasdaya Namah
Om Gunadhyaya Namah
Om Gahanaya Namah
Om Gasthaya Namah
Om Gadya Padya Surdharnavaya
    Namah
Om Gadya Gaan Priyaya Namah
Om Garjaya Namah
Om Geetgirvanapurvajaya Namah
Om Ghyachaarrataya Namah

Om Ghuyhaya Namah
Om Ghuyagamanirupitaya Namah
Om Ghuyashaya Namah
Om Ghuabdhisyay Namah
Om Gurugmahavaya Namay
Om Gurorgurve Namah
Om Ghantaghargharikamaline Namah
Om Ghatkumbhaya Namah
Om Ghatodharaya Namah
Om Chandaya Namah
Om Chandeshwar Surude Namah
Om Chandishaya Namah
Om Chand Vikramaya Namah
Om Characharpatye Namah
Om Chintamani Charvanlalsaya
    Namah
Om Chandse Namah
Om Chandvopuse Namah
Om Chandodurlakshaya Namah
Om Chandvighrahaya Namah
Om Jagadhdyonaye Namah
Om Jagadhshakshine Namah
Om Jagadishaya Namah
Om Jagan Mayaya Namah
Om Japaya Namah
Om Japparaya Namah
Om Japyaya Namah
Om Jhinvasimnhasanaprabhve Namah
Om Zhalazalolsadanazhankaribhramara
    Kulaya Namah
Om Tanzhankarspharsauravaya Namah
Om Tanzhankarmaninupuraya Namah
Om Tadhvipallavanthansta Sarva
    Namah
Om Mantrek Siddhidaya Naman
Om Dindimundaya Namah
Om Dakinishaya Namah
Om Damraya Namah
Om Dindimpriyaya Namah
Om Dhakkaninadmuditaya Namah
Om Dhaukaya Namah
Om Dhundi Vinayakaya Namah
Om Tatvanaampramayatatvaya Namah
Om Tatvampadnirupitaya Namah
Om Tarkantkaya Namah
Om Tarkaya Namah
Om Tarkantkaya Namah
Om Sthanway Namah
Om Sthanupriyaya Namah

Om Sthattre Namah
Om Sthavarayajungmayajagte Namah
Om Daksha Yadhapramathnaya
    Namah
Om Daatre Namah
Om Danvamohanaya Namah
Om Daya Vatye Namah
Om Divya Vibhayaya Namah
Om Dandabhrute Namah
Om Dandanayakaya Namah
Om Dattaprabhinnabhramalaya
    Namah
Om Dyatya Vaarnadarnaya Namah
Om Drastamlagnadvipghataya Namah
Om Devartha Nrugjakrutye Namah
Om Dhandhanyapatye Namah
Om Dhanyaya Namah
Om Dhandaya Namah
Om Dharnidharaya Namah
Om Dhanyekprakataya Namah
Om Dhyeyaya Namah
Om Dhyanaya Namah
Om Dhyanparayanya Namah
Om Nandyaya Namah
Om Nandipriya Namah
Om Nadaya Namah
Om Nadmadhyaprathistaya Namah
Om Niskalaya Namah
Om Nirmalaya Namah
Om Nityaya Namah
Om Nityanityaya Namah
Om Niramayaya Namah
Om Prasmayeyomne Namah
Om Parasmayedhamne Namah
Om Parmatmanye Namah
Om Parasmayepadaya Namah
Om Paratparaya Namah
Om Pashupatye Namah
Om Pashupashvimochakaya Namah
Om Purnanandaya Namah
Om Paranandaya Namah
Om Puranpuroshtamaya Namah

Om Padmaprasnyenaya Namah
Om Prantanyanmochanaya Namah
Om Pramanpratyatiyaya Namah
Om Pranatatinivarnaya Namah
Om Phalhastaya Namah
Om Phanipatye Namah
Om Phetkaraya Namah
Om Phanitpriyaya Namah
Om Baanarchitangiyugulaya Namah
Om Baalkelikutuhaline Namah
Om Brahmane Namah
Om Brahmarchitpadaya Namah
Om Brahmachaarine Namah
Om Bhruhaspatye Namah
Om Brihanadayagrayachitkaraya
    Namah
Om Brahmandavalimekhalaya
    Namah
Om Bhrukeshapdatalakshmikaya
    Namah
Om Bhargaya Namah
Om Bhadraya Namah
Om Bhyaphaya Namah
Om Bhagwate Namah
Om Bhagtisulabhaya Namah
Om Bhutidaya Namah
Om Bhutibhushanaya Namah
Om Bhavyaya Namah
Om Bhootalyaya Namah
Om Bhogmadmatmanoramaya
    Namah
Om Mekhlavate Namah
Om Mandagatye Namah
Om Matitkamalekshanaya Namah
Om Yadhnyaya Namah
Om Yadhnyapatye Namah
Om Yadnyagoptre Namah
Om Yandnyaphalpradaya Namah
Om Yashaskaraya Namah
Om Yogagamyaya Namah
Om Yagnikaya Namah
Om Yachakapriyaya Namah
Om Rasaya Namah
Om Raspriyaya Namah
Om Rasyaya Namah
Om Ranjkaya Namah
Om Ravanarchitaya Namah
Om Rajorakshakaraya Namah
Om Rathnagharbhaya Namah

Om Rajyasukhpradya Namah
Om Lakshaya Namah
Om Lakshapradaya Namah
Om Lakshaya Namah
Om Layasthaya Namah
Om Laddukpriyaya Namah
Om Laasyaparaya Namah
Om Labhkullokavishrutaya Namah
Om Varanyaya Namah
Om Vannivadanaya Namah
Om Varanyaya Namah
Om Vannivddanaya Namah
Om Vannyaya Namah
Om Vedantgocharaya Namah
Om Vedangocharaya Namah
Om Vikarne Namah
Om Vishwataschyachakshushe Namah
Om Vidhatre Namah
Om Vishwatomukhaya Namah
Om Vaamdevaya Namah
Om Vishwanetre Namah
Om Vajrivajranivanaya Namah
Om Vishwabandhanvishakambha-
    dharaya Namah
Om Vishweswarprabhave Namah
Om Shabdhabrahmne Namah
Om Shamprapyaya Namah
Om Shambhushaktiganeshwaraya
    Namah
Om Shastre Namah
Om Shikhagranilaya Namah
Om Sharanyaya Namah
Om Shikreswaraya Namah
Om Shadhrutukusumastragvine
    Namah
Om Shadadharaya Namah
Om Shadaksharaya Namah
Om Sausarnandaya Namah
Om Saruvadnaya Namah
Om Sarvbheshejbhesjaya Namah
Om Srushtistitilayakridaya Namah
Om Srukunjarbhednaya Namah
Om Sindhuritmahakumbhaya Namah

Om Sadsvayadktidayakaya Namah
Om Sakshine Namah
Om Samuradamanthanaya Namah
Om Svaswamvedyaya Namah
Om Svadakshinaya Namah
Om Swatantraya Namah
Om Satyasankalpaya Namah
Om Saamgaanartaya Namah
Om Sukhine Namah
Om Havsaya Namah
Om Hastipisachisaya Namah
Om Havanaya Namah
Om Havyakavyabhuje Namah
Om Havyaya Namah
Om Hutatpriyaya Namah
Om Harshaya Namah
Om Halekhamantramadhyagaya
    Namah
Om Kshetradhipaya Namah
Om Shamabharte Namah
Om Shamaparparayanaya Namah
Om Shiprakshemkaraya Namah
Om Shemanandaya Namah
Om Shonisurdhrubhaya Namah
Om Dharmapadaya Namah
Om Arthdaya Namah
Om Kaamdaatre Namah
Om Saubhagyavardhanaya Namah
Om Vidyapradaya Namah
Om Vibhavdaya Namah
Om Bhukimuktiphalpradaya Namah
Om Aabhirupyakaraya Namah
Om Virshripradaya Namah
Om Vijaypradaya Namah
Om Sarvavashyakaraya Namah
Om Garbhadoshghne Namah
Om Putra Pautradaya Namah
Om Medhadaya Namah
Om Kirtidaya Namah
Om Shokhanine Namah
Om Dorbhagyanaashinaya Namah
Om Prativadimukhastambhaya Namah
Om Rushtachiprasadnaya Namah
Om Parabhichaarshamnaya Namah
Om Dukhbhanjankarkaya Namah
Om Lavaya Namah
Om Trute Namah
Om Kalaye Namah
Om Kastaye Namah

Om Nimishaya Namah
Om Tatparaya Namah
Om Kshanaya Namah
Om Ghataye Namah
Om Muhurtaye Namah
Om Praharaya Namah
Om Diva Namah
Om Nakta Namah
Om Aharnisham Namah
Om Pakshaya Namah
Om Masaya Namah
Om Ayanaya Namah
Om Varshay Namah
Om Yugaya Namah
Om Kalpaya Namah
Om Mahalaya Namah
Om Rashaye Namah
Om Taraye Namah
Om Tithaye Namah
Om Yogaya Namah
Om Varaya Namah
Om Karnaya Namah
Om Aaunshakaya Namah
Om Lagnaya Namah
Om Horayaye Namah
Om Kaalchakraya Namah
Om Merve Namah
Om Saptarshibhyo Namah
Om Dhruvaya Namah
Om Rahave Namah
Om Mandaya Namah
Om Kavye Namah
Om Jiyaya Namah
Om Budhaya Namah
Om Bhaumaya Namah
Om Shashine Namah
Om Rayaye Namah
Om Kalaya Namah
Om Shrustye Namah
Om Sthitye Namah
Om Vishwasthavarjungmanchyate
    Namah
Om Bhuve Namah
Om Adrupbhyo Namah
Om Agnaye Namah
Om Marute Namah
Om Vyomne Namah
Om Ahangkrutye Namah
Om Prakrutye Namah

Om Punse Namah
Om Brahmne Namah
Om Vishnawe Namah
Om Shivaya Namah
Om Rudraya Namah
Om Ishaya Namah
Om Shaktye Namah
Om Sadashivaya Namah
Om Tridashebhyo Namah
Om Pitrubhyo Namah
Om Yakshyebhyo Namah
Om Rakshyobhyo Namah
Om Kinnarebhyo Namah
Om Sadhyebhyo Namah
Om Vidyadharebhyo Namah
Om Bhootebhyo Namah
Om Manyushebhyo Namah
Om Pashubhyo Namah
Om Khagebhyo Namah
Om Samudrebhyo Namah
Om Saridhhyo Namah
Om Shailebhyo Namah
Om Bhootaya Namah
Om Bhavyaya Namah
Om Bhavodbhavaya Namah
Om Sanghkhyaya Namah
Om Patanjalaya Namah
Om Yogaya Namah
Om Puranebhyo Namah
Om Shrutye Namah
Om Smrutye Namah
Om Vedangebhyo Namah
Om Sadachaaraya Namah
Om Mimawsaye Namah
Om Nyayvistaraya Namah
Om Ayurvedaya Namah
Om Dhanurvedaya Namah
Om Gandharvaya Namah
Om Kavyanatkaya Namah
Om Vaikhansaya Namah
Om Bhagvataya Namah
Om Satvataya Namah
Om Pancharankaya Namah
Om Shaivaya Namah
Om Pashupataya Namah
Om Kaalmukhaya Namah
Om Bhairavshsanaya Namah
Om Shaaktaya Namah
Om Vainayakaya Namah

Om Sauraya Namah
Om Jainaya Namah
Om Aahantasaunhitaya Namah
Om Satye Namah
Om Aasatye Namah
Om Vyaktaya Namah
Om Ayaktaya Namah
Om Sachetnaya Namah
Om Achetnaya Namah
Om Vandhaya Namah
Om Mokshaya Namah
Om Sukhaya Namah
Om Bhogaya Namah
Om Ayogaya Namah
Om Satyaya Namah
Om Aanve Namah
Om Mahate Namah
Om Swasit Namah
Om Hu Namah
Om Fannum Namah
Om Svadha Namah
Om Svaha Namah
Om Shraushnaam Namah
Om Vowshnaam Namah
Om Vashanaam Namah
Om Namo Namah
Om Nyanaya Namah
Om Vidnyanaya Namah
Om Anandaya Namah
Om Bodhaya Namah
Om Savanvide Namah
Om Shamaya Namah
Om Yamaya Namah
Om Ekasmaye Namah
Om Ekashdharaya Namah
Om Ekashparanarayanaya Namah
Om Ekagradhiye Namah
Om Ekviraya Namah
Om Ekanekswaroopdhrushe Namah
Om Dwi Rupaya Namah
Om Dwi Bhujaya Namah
Om Vyadhakshaya Namah
Om Dwirdaya Namah
Om Dwipvakshakaya Namah
Om Dwematuraya Namah
Om Dwidnaya Namah

Om Dwandantitaya Namah

Om Dwayatigaya Namah
Om Tridhamne Namah
Om Trikaraya Namah
Om Tretatrivargaphaldaya Namah
Om Trigunatmane Namah
Om Trilokdaye Namah
Om Trishaktishaya Namah
Om Trilochanaya Namah
Om Chaturbhaharve Namah
Om Chatudantarnaya Namah
Om Chaturtamane Namah
Om Chaturmukhaya Namah
Om Chatuvirdhopayamayaya Namah
Om Chaturvarnashramashraya Namah
Om Chatu Virdhav Chovrutti
    Parivruttipravartkaya Namah
Om Chaturthi Pujan Pritaya Namah
Om Chaturthi Tithi Sambhavaya
    Namah
Om Panchaksharatmane Namah
Om Panchatmane Namah
Om Panchasyaya Namah
Om Panchkrutyakrute Namah
Om Panchadharaya Namah
Om Panchavaranaya Namah
Om Panchaksharparayanaya Namah
Om Panchtalaya Namah
Om Panchkaraya Namah
Om Panchpranavbhavitaya Namah
Om PPanchbhramayasphurtye Namah
Om Panchavaranvaritaya Namah
Om Panchbhakshapriyaya Namah
Om Panchbanaya Namah
Om Panchshivatmakaya Namah
Om Shastakonpithaya Namah
Om Shastachakradhamne Namah
Om Shastagranithbhedakaya Namah
Om Shadadhvadhvantvidhwansine
    Namah

Om Shandgulmahahryadaya Namah
Om Shanmukhaya Namah
Om Shanmukhbhrave Namah
Om Shastashakliparivaritaya Namah
Om Shadavairivargvidhwansine Namah
Om Shadamirbhayabhanjanaya Namah
Om Shastatkarduraya Namah
Om Shastakarmanirtaya Namah
Om Shadrashasraya Namah
Om Saptapatalcharanaya Namah
Om Saptadviporupmandalaya Namah
Om Saptaswarlokmukutaya Namah
Om Saptangrajyasukhdaya Namah
Om Saptarshiganmanditaya Namah
Om Saptachandonidhye Namah
Om Saptahotre Namah
Om Saptasvarashraya Namah
Om Saptadhikelikasaraya Namah
Om Saptagatrunishevitaya Namah
Om Saptachandomodmadaya Namah
Om Saptachandomakhphrabhve
    Namah
Om Aastamurtidheyamurtye Namah
Om Aastaprakurtikarnaya Namah
Om Aastangyogphalbhuve Namah
Om Aastpatrambujasanaya Namah
Om Aasstashaktisamrudhishriye
    Namah
Om Aashtayeaishwariyapradykaya
    Namah
Om Aastaphitopphitshriye Namah
Om Aastamatrusamavrutaya Namah
Om Aastabhairavsevvyaya Namah
Om Aastavasuvandhaya Namah
Om Aastamurtibhrute Namah
Om Aastachakrasphuranmurtye Namah
Om Aastadravyahavimpriyaaya Namah
Om Navnagasanadhyasine Namah
Om Navnidhyanushasitre Namah

Om Navdwarpuradharaya Namah
Om Navadharniketanaya Namah
Om Navnarayanshitaya Namah
Om Navdurganishevitaya Namah
Om Navanathmahanathaya Namah
Om Navnagvibhusnaya Namah
Om Navratnavichitrangaya Namah
Om Navshaktishirodhrutaya Namah
Om Dashatmakaya Namah
Om Dashabhujaya Namah
Om Dashadikapativanditaya Namah
Om Dashadhyayaya Namah
Om Dashapranaya Namah
Om Dashendriyaamkaya Namah
Om Dashaksharmahamantraya Namah
Om Dashashavyapivigrahaya Namah
Om Ekadashadibhirudremstutaya
    Namah
Om Ekadashaksharaya Namah
Om Dwadashdandadodarndaya Namah
Om Dwadshantaniketanaya Namah
Om Trayodasbhidabhinna-
    vishwedevadhidevataya Namah
Om Chatushendravardaya Namah
Om Chatudarshamanuprabhave
    Namah
Om Chatudarshadividyadhyaya Namah
Om Chatudarshajagatprabhave Namah
Om Saampanchdashaya Namah
Om Panchadashshitanshunimarlaya
    Namah
Om Shodadarnilaya Namah
Om Shodasswarmatrukaya Namah
Om Prodshantpadvasaya namah
Om Shodshendukalamakaya Namah
Om Kaalsaptadashye Namah
Om Saptadashaya Namah
Om Saptadashaksharaya Namah
Om Aashtadashdvippatye Namah
Om Aastadashapurankrute Namah
Om Aastadashosdhisrustye Namah
Om Aastadashvidhismrutaya Namah
Om Aashtadashalipiyashtimsamis-
    thanyankovidaya Namah
Om Ekvinshayapunse Namah
Om Ekvinshtyangullipallavaya Namah
Om Chatuvirshatitatvatmane Namah

Om Panchvinshashakyapurshaya Namah

Om Saptavinshanitareshaya Namah

Om Saptavinshantiyogkrute Namah

Om Dwatrinshatbhairavadhishaya Namah

Om Chatunishtrashanmamahahridaya Namah

Om Shastatrinshattatvasambhootye Namah

Om Aastatrinshatkalanatve Namah

Om Namodekonpanchashanmarud-varganirgarlaya Namah

Om Panchashdaksharshrenye Namah

Om Panchasdrudravigrahaya Namah

Om Panchasdvishnushaktishaya Namah

Om Panchashamatrukalaya Namah

Om Dvipanchasdvapushrenye Namah

Om Trishastayaksharsanshraya Namah

Om Chatrumshastayarnaninetre Namah

Om Chatushshastikalridhye Namah

Om Chatushshastimahasiddhiyo-ginivrindhvanditaya Namah

Om Aastashastimahatrithshek-trabhairavbhavanaya Namah

Om Chaturnarvatimantratmane Namah

Om Shaanvatyadhikphrabhave Namah

Om Shantanandaya Namah

Om Shatdhrutye Namah

Om Shatpatrayatekshanaya Namah

Om Shatanikaya Namah

Om Shatmakhaya Namah

Om Shatdharavyudhaya Namah

Om Sahastrapatranilaya Namah

Om Sahastraphanmushnaya Namah

Om Sahastrashirnepurshaya Namah

Om Sahastrashakashaya Namah

Om Sahastrapadye Namah

Om Sahastranaamsanstutaya Namah

Om Sahastrakshapalapahaya Namah

Om Dashasahastraphanbhritpha-niraajkrutasanaya Namah

Om Aastashitisahastrayadh-maharshistotrayanitrataya Namah

Om Lakshadishpriyadhavaya Namah

Om Lakshadharmanomayaya Namah

Om Chaturlakshaprakashitaya Namah

Om Chaturlakshajappritaya Namah

Om Chaturshitilakshana-jivanadehsansthitaya Namah

Om Kotisuryapratikashaya Namah

Om Kotichandrashunirmalaya Namah

Om Shivabhavadhyustako-tivinayakdhurandharaya Namah

Om Saptakotimahamantramanitra-tavayadhyute Namah

Om Trayasintrashatkotisurshreni-pranatpadukaya Namah

Om Anantatmane Namah

Om Anantshriye Namah

Om Harasunave Namah

Om Guhagrajaya Namah

Om Ekadantaya Namah

Om Gajadantaya Namah

Om Batave Namah

Om Suragranyaya Namah

Om Chaturbhujaya Namah

Om Vinayakaya Namah

Om Sarvesvaraya Namah

|| Om Anantantant Soukhya Daya Namah ||
|| Shri Guru Ganesharpanmastu ||